Thinking and Acting Like a

Behavioral School Counselor

*For Esti, Deana, Nicole and Mimi . . . four strong,
talented, and accomplished women, whom I love.*

RICHARD D. PARSONS

Thinking and Acting Like a Behavioral School Counselor

CORWIN
A SAGE Company

Cover Art "Galactic Storms" by Lucy Arnold www.lucyarnold.com

For information:

Corwin
A SAGE Company
2455 Teller Road
Thousand Oaks, California 91320
(800) 233-9936
Fax: (800) 417-2466
www.corwinpress.com

SAGE India Pvt. Ltd.
B 1/I 1 Mohan Cooperative
   Industrial Area
Mathura Road, New Delhi 110 044
India

SAGE Ltd.
1 Oliver's Yard
55 City Road
London EC1Y 1SP
United Kingdom

SAGE Asia-Pacific Pte. Ltd.
33 Pekin Street #02-01
Far East Square
Singapore 048763

Printed in the United States of America.

Library of Congress Cataloging-in-Publication Data

Parsons, Richard D.
Thinking and acting like a behavioral school counselor/Richard D. Parsons.
     p. cm.
Includes bibliographical references and index.
ISBN 978-1-4129-6650-4 (cloth)
ISBN 978-1-4129-6651-1 (pbk.)

   1. Educational counseling. 2. Student counselors. 3. Problem children—Behavior modification. I. Title.

LB1027.5.P319 2009
371.4—dc22   2009002810

This book is printed on acid-free paper.

09   10   11   12   13   10   9   8   7   6   5   4   3   2   1

Acquisitions Editor:	Arnis Burvikovs
Associate Editor:	Desirée A. Bartlett
Production Editor:	Eric Garner
Copy Editor:	Gretchen Treadwell
Typesetter:	C&M Digitals (P) Ltd.
Proofreader:	Carole Quandt
Indexer:	Jean Casalegno
Cover Designer:	Michael Dubowe

Contents

Preface

Thinking and Acting Like a Behavioral School Counselor

As the title of this text may suggest, the pages that follow will provide descriptions and illustrations of the use of various behavioral strategies, including the performance of functional behavioral analyses, the use of operant conditioning, and various other similar procedures. But this is only part of the focus of this text.

The unique value of *Thinking and Acting Like a Behavioral School Counselor* is that it goes beyond the presentation of a theory and assists the readers to step into that theory, embrace it as an organizational framework and then—and most importantly—employ it to guide their procedural thinking when confronted with client information.

TEXT FORMAT AND CHAPTER STRUCTURE

Procedural knowledge, or the ability to know what to do when the student does this or that, is a hallmark of the expert counselor. Research suggests that procedural knowledge is acquired as the result of practice accompanied by feedback. Practice and feedback will be central to this text.

Case illustrations, case presentations with analyses of counselor actions and the decision-making processes underlying them, along with guided-practice activities, will be employed as "teaching tools" throughout the text. The book will be organized around the following parts. Part I introduces the reader to a reflective practitioner model of school counseling (Chapter 1) and the fundamentals of a behavioral orientation (Chapter 2). With these as foundations, Part II provides the reader with specific behavioral interventions targeting the development of desired behavior (Chapter 3), the reduction of undesirable behaviors (Chapter 4), and the replacement of behavior by way of counterconditioning (Chapter 5).

The final part of the book, Part III, invites the reader to first "observe" the thinking of a school counselor operating from a behavioral-orienting framework (Chapter 6) and then to actually apply a behavioral-orienting framework to case materials (Chapter 7).

As with all texts of this nature, this book is but a beginning. For school counselors, embracing the value and efficacy of a behavioral framework to guide their reflective practice additional training, supervision and professional development is a must. Hopefully, *Thinking and Acting Like a Behavioral School Counselor* provides a good springboard to that end.

—RDP

Acknowledgments

As with each of the books in this series, while I have been credited with the authorship of this text, many others have significantly contributed to the formation and shaping of my thoughts into the text you hold in your hands. First, I want to thank Arnis Burvikovs at Corwin for encouraging me to pursue this book series, and Desirée Bartlett and Eric Garner for the ongoing support throughout the project. I would like to acknowledge the support and encouragement I have received from my colleagues, particularly Naijian Zhang, Wally Kahn, and Charles Good. I sincerely appreciate the hard work and editorial support provided to me by my graduate assistant, Erica Morrison, and a special "thank you" to Gretchen Treadwell for helping my thoughts take shape in the King's best English. Finally, I would like to publicly thank my wife, Ginny, not only for her professional insights, but also for her ongoing affirmation and support.

—RDP

Corwin gratefully acknowledges the contributions of the following individuals:

Leah M. Rouse Arndt, Clinical Assistant Professor
University of Wisconsin, Milwaukee
Milwaukee, WI

Cynthia Knowles, Prevention Specialist
Livonia Central School District
Livonia, NY

William Livers, School Social Worker
SW Parke Community Schools District
Montezuma, IN

Katy Olweiler, Counselor
Lakeside School
Seattle, WA

Diane Smith, School Counselor
Smethport Area School District
Smethport, PA

About the Author

© 2008 John Shetron

Richard D. Parsons, PhD, is a full professor in the Department of Counseling and Educational Psychology at West Chester University in Eastern Pennsylvania. Dr. Parsons has over thirty-two years of university teaching in counselor preparation programs. Prior to his university teaching, Dr. Parsons spent nine years as a school counselor in an inner-city high school. Dr. Parsons has been the recipient of many awards and honors, including the Pennsylvania Counselor of the Year award.

Dr. Parsons has authored or coauthored over eighty professional articles and books. His most recent books include the texts: *Counseling Strategies That Work! Evidenced-Based for School Counselors* (2006), *The School Counselor as Consultant* (2004), *Teacher as Reflective Practitioner and Action Researcher* (2001), *Educational Psychology* (2001), *The Ethics of Professional Practice* (2000), *Counseling Strategies and Intervention Techniques* (1994), and *The Skills of Helping* (1995). In addition to these texts, Dr. Parsons has authored or coauthored three seminal works in the area of psycho-educational consultation, *Mental Health Consultation in the Schools* (1993), *Developing Consultation Skills* (1985), and *The Skilled Consultant* (1995).

Dr. Parsons has a private practice and serves as a consultant to educational institutions and mental health service organizations throughout the tri-state area. Dr. Parsons has served as a national consultant to the Council of Independent Colleges in Washington, DC, providing institutions of higher education with assistance in the areas of program development, student support services, pedagogical innovation and assessment procedures.

Introduction
to Book Series

Transforming Theory Into Practice

There was a time—at least this is what is I've been told—when school counselors were called upon to calm the child who lost his lunch, intervene with two middle school students who were "name calling," and provide guidance to a senior considering college options. Now, I know these tasks are still on school counselors' "things-to-do lists," but a brief review of any one typical day in the life of a school counselor will suggest that these were the good old days!

You do not need the research or statistics on divorce rates, violence, drug use, sexual abuse, etc. to "know" that our society and our children are in crises. Each of the multitude of referrals you receive provides you with abundant evidence of this crisis.

It is not just the increased number of children seeking your assistance that is the issue—it is the increased severity and complexity of problems with which they present. The problems addressed by today's school counselor certainly include "name calling" and teasing, but sadly, in today's society, that form of interaction can quickly escalate to violence involving deadly weapons. Perhaps you still have the child or two who is upset about misplaced lunches—or homework, or jackets—but it is also not unusual to find the upset is grounded in the anticipated abuse that will be received when his or her parent finds out.

School children with significant depression, debilitating anxieties, energy-draining obsessions, damaged self-concepts, and self-destructive behaviors can be found in any school and in any counselor's office throughout our land. Responding to these children in ways that facilitate their development and foster their growth through education is a daunting task for today's school counselor. It is a task that demands a high degree of knowledge, skill, and competency. It is a task that demands effective, efficient translation of theory and research into practice.

1

The current series, *Transforming Theory Into Practice*, provides school counselors practical guides to gathering and processing client data, developing case conceptualizations, and formulating and implementing specific treatment plans. Each book in the series emphasizes skill development and, as such, each book provides extensive case illustrations and guided-practice exercises in order to move the reader from simply "knowing" to "doing."

The expanding needs of our children, along with the demands for increased accountability in our profession, require that each of us continue to sharpen our knowledge and skills as helping professionals. It is the hope that the books presented within this series, *Transforming Theory Into Practice*, facilitate your own professional development and support you in your valued work of counseling our children.

Part I

Using Behavioral Orientation to Guide Reflection

For school counselors, a behavioral approach to counseling is neither new nor novel. With application to classroom management and many—if not most—of the problems presented by our students, a behavioral approach to school counseling has been demonstrated to be both pragmatic and efficacious. However, for behavioral theory to be of real value to the school counselor, it must be assimilated and employed as a framework to guide practice, conceptualization, and decision making.

For the school counselor, the real value of this, or any, theory or model of counseling is in its potential to facilitate the process of gathering student information, discerning what is important from what is not, and knowing what needs to be done to move the student from the "what is" to the "what is desired." The information found within Part I highlights the value of a behavioral model to guide the reflection and decision making of the school counselor. Chapter 1 introduces the reader to the concept of reflective practice as a process shaping the decisions and actions of the effective school counselor. Chapter 2 outlines the fundamental principles and constructs of a behavioral approach to school counseling as a valuable orientating framework to guide this reflective practice.

The School Counselor as Reflective Practitioner

1

"No I'm not going. I can't go. Please, please don't make me go! Please . . . please, I'll do anything you want."

—William P., eight years old[1]

The anguish conveyed by William's plea to stay home rather than go to school speaks to the intensity of his experience. However, this simple disclosure provides little insight into why this process of attending school would elicit such a strong, aversive response—or, more importantly, what the counselor could do to reduce this anguish.

Perhaps as you read the above you began to generate a number of "hypotheses" about what may be going on . . . and what needs to be done. As school counselors, we do not, nor can we, sit as simple passive recipients of comments such as these. Our job, our calling, is to do more than listen. While trained to be good listeners, we know that listening is but the vehicle to understanding, and that understanding is the base from which we formulate our helping strategies.

A statement such as that provided by William invites the school counselor into a process of reflection and search for meaning. Through the process of reflection, the school counselor identifies what is important from what is not, understands the "what is" and the "what is hoped for," and develops connections that will guide the student to this desired outcome.

For example, a counselor hearing William's plea may attempt to discern whether this is a manifestation of panic—or perhaps, the manipulation of a child who has found such pleas to be effective strategies for gaining a day off from school. Perhaps the school counselor questions the possibility of the existence of noxious experiences encountered in school, which may serve as the impetus for this resistance. Is there bullying occurring? Is the child misplaced and thus feeling like a failure? Or, are there concerns about what may be going on at home while the child is away at school? What is the nature of the relationship of his parents? How is the health of his mother? What is his role in the family? These reflections, these internal questions, serve as the bases from which the counselor's actions and interventions emerge.

The ability to listen—receive, and most importantly, make meaning out of the student's disclosure—is essential to the helping process. While the current text focuses upon the use of a behavioral-orienting framework to guide these processes, it is important to first understand the value of this reflection and meaning making to all counselors, regardless of theoretical orientation.

REFLECTIVE PRACTICE

The processes of *attending to* and then *responding to* our students' information are linked by our ability to reflect on these data. The counselor engaged in the dynamic of a counseling relationship is engaged in a search, a reflective process. It is a process that will give direction to the way he or she responds to any one student, at any one moment in a counseling session as he or she attempts to facilitate movement from the "what is" to the "what is desired."

Reflection on our counseling has been identified as an essential component to effective practice (Nelson & Neufeldt, 1998). To be successful, a school counselor has to have the ability to scrutinize the nature and impact of his or her interventions—both at the macro level (e.g., in developing a treatment plan) and at the micro level (e.g., with each interactive exchange in a counseling session).

Reflection at the Global Level: Case Conceptualization

Unlike the counselor-in-training who may find him- or herself overwhelmed by client disclosure and unclear where or how to proceed, the effective school counselor is able to navigate through student disclosures in order to identify those data that are significant from those data that are superfluous. It is clear that not all client information is of equal value or importance to the process and outcome of the counseling. The effective school counselor reflects on the student's disclosures and formulates these data into a coherent, yet tentative, conceptualization of what is, what is desired, and how to move from "A" to "B." This ability to conceptualize *"what is"* in terms of presenting concerns and the student's resources and the *"what is hoped for,"* as the goals and outcomes for the counseling, sets the framework for consideration of strategies and techniques needed to move the student toward the desired outcome. With this conceptualization in mind, the counselor will call upon previous experience as well as knowledge of current research to begin the selection of the strategies to be employed.

Perhaps a school counselor has worked with numerous students who present as "nonmotivated," and as a result, have failing grades. While the problem is labeled with the same term, "nonmotivated," the cause for this lack of motivation is idiosyncratic to each student and thus the intervention employed must similarly be shaped in response to the uniqueness of that individual. The effective school counselor reflects upon the data at his or her disposal to shape the best intervention possible for any one student at any one time.

This planning and reflection is not a static, one-time process—rather, it refers to the thinking that takes place following a session or an encounter. This then allows the counselor to review what he or she did, what was anticipated to happen, and what in fact happened. From the initial meeting through to the ending of any one "contract," the effective school counselor must gather and analyze case information, formulate new hypotheses, and develop and implement intervention decisions.

The reflective counselor will observe the effect of his or her intervention and collect data, either formal or anecdotal, in order to test the observed outcome against what was hypothesized. Taking time to reflect upon and consider the "experience" of the session helps provide data from which to judge the direction the sessions are taking, the rate with which the student is moving in the desired direction, and even helps the counselor develop a set of questions, ideas, and propositions to be tested in the next encounter. This reflection "on" practice allows the counselor to refine the case conceptualization and reframe the direction of the strategies employed. This process of reflection "on" practice is depicted in Figure 1.1, and further illustrated by the following case.

Figure 1.1   Reflection "on" Practice

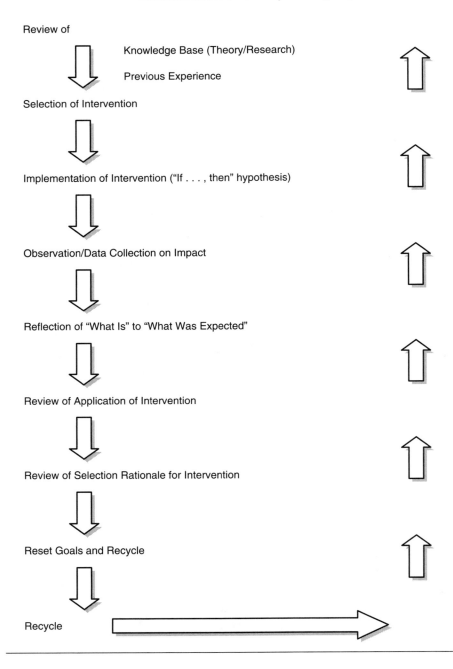

Rick, a bright, successful and well-liked eleventh-grade student, came to counseling seeking assistance with his college selection process. Having served as Rick's counselor since his entrance into the school in ninth grade, Mr. "P" felt that he had a good handle on Rick and had established an excellent working relationship. With these historic data as his bases, Mr. P approached the session with the intent of directing Rick to the self-search program as an initial step to identifying a pool of colleges of interest (*Step 1: Identification of goal [or subgoal]*). In preparing to develop a treatment plan, the counselor relied on two sources of knowledge (*Step 2: Review of knowledge base/experience*):

a. A review of Rick's cumulative folder revealed that he was an honor's student; successful athlete lettering in both varsity basketball and football; and a star socially, being class president and voted "homecoming king." Rick's mom and dad were both successful professionals (mom, a physician, and dad, a CEO of a financial company) and were very supportive of Rick, their eldest son.

b. Prior to meeting with Rick, Mr. P reviewed Rick's interest inventory noting that he had consistently expressed an interest in medicine, and as such, Mr. P researched universities which had good track records placing students in medical schools.

With this information as the knowledge base, Mr. P proposed that Rick start with a listing of highly competitive and competitive schools, and with the aid of the computerized self-search program review university descriptions, requirements, etc. (*Step 3: Selection of intervention*). The plan was enacted using the following steps (*Step 4: Intervention implementation*):

a. First, Mr. P explained the search process.

b. Rick sat and simply "played" with program options as Mr. P provided instruction and support.

c. Once comfortable with the program, Rick would use his study hall over the course of the next two weeks to begin to identify universities "of interest," which he and Mr. P would review, together.

Both Mr. P and Rick felt good about the program and thus it was implemented. Over the course of the next couple of days, Rick would come to the counseling office during his study period, and after saying hi to Mr. P, would proceed to the career center and the self-directed search. Early in the second week, when Rick stopped in, Mr. P greeted him and asked, "How is it going?" Rick's response, while stating "okay," was couched in a tone and body language that suggested it was anything but okay! (*Step 4: Observation and data collection*).

While Mr. P had anticipated that, by this point in the process, Rick would be getting excited about his finds, the lack of enthusiasm was significant (*Step 5: Comparison of "what is" to "what was expected"*). Sitting with Rick, it was clear he had no problem using the self-directed search and in fact was able to read about a variety of university programs, thus the initial "intervention" was implemented (*Step 6: Review of application*) and it should have worked, given the counselor's experience and the extensive supportive research (*Step 7: Review rationale*). The question of course is, "why wasn't it?" Why wasn't Rick becoming excited and more focused on specific programs? (*Step 8: Reset goals and recycle.*)

As a result of meeting with Rick and asking him about his experience, it became clear that finding a specific college of choice was *not* the desired goal. Rather, Rick began to share that he really wasn't sure that he wanted to go to college right after graduation, but felt that this would devastate his parents and as such, he was becoming increasingly anxious and depressed about having to do something he truly did not want to do. As evidenced by this case illustration, an essential component to our reflection "on" practice is our awareness of movement toward desired outcome. Reflecting "on" these new data resulted in the resetting of the goals of counseling and the interventions to be employed.

Reflection at the Microlevel: Reflection "in" Process

Counseling is a dynamic process. Engaging with a student in a helping relationship cannot be staged in nice linear steps. A school counselor may come to a session prepared with a "plan" and a toolbox of wonderful interventions. However, while having a clear sense of both what is and what is needed is essential to be an effective counselor, school counselors know things rarely go as planned.

Being aware that at any one moment things are not as one expects, and allowing those data and that awareness to guide adjustments in the process, is another time when a counselor needs to rely on reflective practice. This time, however, the reflection occurs in the session and quite often on the fly.

This process of reflection in practice is a complex metacognitive process that happens very quickly and most often below the counselor's immediate level of awareness. A simple illustration of reflection "in" process can be found in the activity of riding a bike. While a person may be a "seasoned" bike rider, having previously successfully balanced the two wheel vehicle and joyfully proceeded down a park pathway, the experience of encountering loose gravel as he or she begins to turn a corner may demand some adjustment to move from what is (i.e., sliding) to what is desired (i.e., upright riding). Becoming aware of a number of unexpected events—for example, the bike leaning too far left, or the sound of wheels slipping, or the sensation of falling—will serve as data that stimulates the rider to adjust and shift body weight and perhaps begin a slow process of breaking. Each of these adjustments in response to the awareness of the new and unexpected direction the bike riding appears to be taking allows the rider to right the process and return to the desired joyful ride. This is *reflection in process*. It is a process that occurs quickly and perhaps only as a result of after-the-fact reflection—knowingly. It is a process that can be learned. It is a process we need to nurture in order to be more effective within our moment-to-moment interactions with our students.

Counseling as a reflective process is one in which the counselor is simultaneously involved in design and implementation of action, "[. . .] while at the same time remaining detached enough to observe and feel the action that is occurring, and to respond" (Tremmel, 1993, p. 436). Consider the simple example of offering a tissue to a tearful student. What is the intent of such a gesture? While such a gesture appears perhaps caring and helpful, might it signal that tears are not allowed? Could offering the tissue highlight and thus sensitize a student who feels somewhat embarrassed by the tears? Are these the purpose of the activity?

The counselor who is reflective knows what he or she expected to achieve by this gesture and will rapidly process the student's reactions, contrasting it to what was expected and adjusting accordingly. Therefore, the counselor who is providing the tissue as invitation to share feelings may note the student's dismissal of that invitation and in turn simply state, "Ginny, you seem upset. Would you like to tell me what's going on?" Or, perhaps the counselor is offering the tissues as a simple physical comfort but notes that the client becomes embarrassed by the counselor's recognition of the apparent upset. Under these conditions, the counselor may simply lower the box and place it on the table, redirecting the student with the comment, "Ginny, I'm glad you are here. Have a seat [pointing to a chair] and make yourself comfortable." These are not actions that can be prescribed nor even anticipated, but require that rapid processing of data and comparison of what is to what was hoped for, with the result being an adjustment of counselor action.

As may be apparent from the brief illustrations, reflection in practice is often stimulated by the counselor's experience of dissonance and emotional discomfort in response to an exchange. Whether it is the student's unexpected embarrassment when offered a tissue box, or the strong resistance and denial in response to the counselor's "therapeutic" confrontation, the experience of what is when conflicting with what was expected creates the dissonance and discomfort that stimulates reflection in practice. With this discomfort as the stimulant for reflection, the counselor will critically (although nonjudgmentally) analyze the initial assumptions and beliefs about the student and the processes being employed.

Consider the case of the counselor working with Lisa, an eighth grader who was sent to the counselor because she was being "disrespectful" to her Spanish teacher. Having previously worked with Lisa and feeling that she had a strong, trusting relationship, Ms. "D" attempted to confront Lisa when she stated, "I didn't say or do anything disrespectful. I just told her it wasn't me making the noise!" Ms. D responded, "Lisa, I know you said you simply stated it wasn't you making the noise, but even when telling me, you sounded really angry. Is it possible that is how it sounded to Mrs. Johnson and that is what she meant by disrespectful?"

While the hope of this confrontation was to open Lisa to the possibility that it is not just words, but the way they are delivered that may have an impact, the response from Lisa suggested this intervention was ineffective. Lisa stated, emphatically, "No! I said it real nice. Why don't you believe me [said very defensively]?" Clearly, the strength of the relationship or the timing of this confrontation was not right for it to be effective. Surprised by Lisa's reaction, Ms. D neither blamed the student (What's wrong with her?) or became overly self-critical (Blew that one!). Rather, Ms. D attempted to hypothesize about what happened and what she could do next in response. Concluding that Lisa was too defensive at this point to embrace her role in this situation, Ms. D decided to simply encourage her to share her story—and provide Lisa with evidence of her care, concern, and unconditional valuing. It was hoped that as the relationship strengthened, and Lisa had increased evidence of being heard and valued, that then a confrontation may prove effective.

ORIENTING FRAMEWORKS: GUIDING REFLECTION

Essential to reflective practice is the counselor's awareness of a disparity between what is and what is expected. But how does a counselor know what to expect? What are the standards, the measures, against which to contrast actual events? While there are no single set of universal markers of what should be expected at any one point in our counseling, expectations of what "should be" can be established as outgrowth of the counselor's model or orienting framework. Our counseling models not only place the student's issues within a meaningful context, but also establish what to expect when stimuli for change are introduced (Irving & Williams, 1995).

So, prior to making any meaningful reflections and procedural decisions, the effective school counselor needs a framework—a schema or a rough template—that helps him or her make sense of the data being gathered.

WHICH ORIENTATION?

Given the more than 130 extant theories of counseling, is there one or a few that a school counselor should employ? While proponents of various schools of thought may argue the differential value of their particular theories, that type of discussion falls outside of the purpose of this text. The purpose of this book is not the validation of a theory or the analysis of the comparative utility of various theories, rather the purpose and focus taken here it is to demonstrate the impact of employing a particular orienting framework—behavioral—has on the process and outcome of school counseling.

The chapters to follow will introduce you to the theory, philosophy, fundamental concepts, and intervention strategies employed by school counselors operating from a behavioral orientation. However, as stated, the value is not simply in knowing—but in applying and, as such, throughout the chapters, you will be invited to step into a behavioral orienting framework as you reflect on the cases presented and anticipate the decisions to be made.

SUMMARY

Counselors in Search of Meaning

- Listening to student disclosure and attempting to make meaning of those disclosures requires that a school counselor employ a model, a guide, or an orienting framework that places this disclosure into some meaningful context.

Counselor Reflections Guiding Practice

- The counselor's ability to reflect on his or her counseling has been identified as an essential component to effective practice.

(Continued)

(Continued)

- Reflection provides the counselor the means to make sense of all the data presented by a student and to connect those data with a counselor response and interventions.

Orienting Frameworks Guiding Reflection

- A counselor's theory, model, or orienting framework provides the "structure" needed to begin to understand the large amount of information gathered in counseling and use that understanding to formulate effective intervention plans.

NOTE

1. The cases presented represent composites of real students; all names and identifying information have been modified to insure anonymity.

The Fundamentals   **2**
of a Behavioral
Orientation

For many school counselors, who by training or personal inclination have embraced a humanistic perspective of human nature, the thought of approaching counseling from a behavioral perspective may appear simply abhorrent. The intent here is not to argue for a philosophical posture, but rather to demonstrate the value of a behavioral perspective as it guides the practice of school counseling.

There is extensive research demonstrating the efficacy of behavioral interventions for a wide range of problems typically encountered by school counselors (see Parsons, 2007). This research suggests that behavioral interventions are not only effective for clinical issues such as depression (Martell, Addis, & Jacobson, 2001) and anxiety (Whitlock, Orleans, Pender, & Allan, 2002), but are also effective in reducing classroom disruptions (Wilkinson, 2003); increasing attention (Evans, Axelrod, & Langberg, 2004); homework and task completion (Bryan & Sullivan-Burstein, 1998) and academic performance (Duhon et al., 2004).

The existence of this efficacy research supports the need for school counselors to develop an understanding and facility for this approach.

BASIC ASSUMPTIONS

Counseling with a behavioral perspective engages the school counselor in the systematic utilization of observational data and the employment of the scientific method in the development, implementation, and assessment of his or her interventions. In its classic form, the behavioral orientation emphasizes observation and analyses and focuses on overt behavior, without discussion of affect or internal mental states. In addition to valuing the observable and the scientifically validated, the school counselor employing a behavioral-orienting framework embraces the following philosophical assumptions as lenses to view student disclosures and with those disclosures, formulates interventions.

Behaviorism as Naturalistic

A fundamental assumption undergirding a behavioral orientation is that everything, including all human behavior, can be explained in terms of natural laws. The same forces that operate to support the development of healthy achievement needs, social skills, and functional schooling behavior are operating to foster the development of those behaviors which school counselors find so problematic. The student who works to achieve does so because achievement is functional; it serves a purpose. Similarly, the student who "works" to avoid school achievement, by refusing to do homework, cutting class, etc. does so because these behaviors are also functional, serving some purpose for that student. Perhaps, it could be said that the "natural law" operating in both circumstances is that humans engage in functional, purposeful behavior.

Consider the student identified as "unmotivated." While there may be abundant evidence that this student does not engage in the classroom assignments, the question remains, "Is this evidence of the absence of motivation?" Isn't it just as likely that this student has as much motivation as the classroom achiever, but that simply the goal for which this student strives, and thus is motivated to achieve, differs from that desired by his classroom teacher? With this as the perspective, the school counselor would be less concerned with generating motivation within this student and, in contrast, would turn attention to identifying ways that his motivation can be targeted to school activities.

If the "natural law" is that we simply do things that work, that serve a purpose, that in some way satisfy our need, then the directive for this student and this counselor would be to find a way to tie school achievement to this student's needs and satisfaction of those needs.

Behavior Acquired Through Conditioning

Behaviorists, while embracing the influence of genetics, value and highlight the impact of experience—learning or conditioning—in the shaping of our human behavior. As B. F. Skinner declared, "A person does not act upon the world, the world acts upon him" (Skinner, 1971, p. 211). Thus, the position taken by a school counselor with a behavioral perspective would be that a student's behavior is best understood in the context of the experiences that student has and has had along with the associations he or she has made, and the reinforcement contingencies he or she has come to expect. The power of this position is that the counselor embracing this principle views all behaviors—those deemed inappropriate as well as those prized and valued—as products of this fundamental learning and conditioning.

Consider those behaviors such as asking to be excused to use the bathroom, or waiting to be recognized before speaking out, or even the simple process of taking turns. These behaviors, all viewed as socially appropriate and desirable, are not hard-wired at birth. Aren't these all products of our experience, our learning, and our conditioning? If we embrace the position that these "socially appropriate" responses are learned, then it follows that those responses deemed "socially inappropriate" are also learned or perhaps reflect the lack of opportunity to learn what is desirable.

From this perspective, the student presenting with what has been labeled as inappropriate or dysfunctional behavior is simply manifesting a behavior—learned like any other behaviors—and not exhibiting a "symptom" of an underlying disease. Thus, the student who is identified as a bully and who employs aggression as a "skill" to acquire a sense of personal power or recognition does so for the same reason that the scholar studies, or the talented musician, practices . . . it works! While one behavior, bullying, is identified as socially unacceptable, it has been developed and maintained through the same mechanisms that those behaviors we prize have been developed.

Dysfunctional Behavior
Rather Than Pathological Individuals

A very important philosophical assumption with which behavioral counselors approach their work is that they believe that behavior, all behavior, is simply that—behavior. For the behavioral counselor, there is no real qualitative distinction between what we call normal and that labeled abnormal behavior.

With the emphasis on learning and learning experience as the foundations for the development of our behavior, the behavioral counselor assumes that the appropriateness of a particular behavior is a function of its adaptive quality and functionality within a particular context. For example, a student who is walking down the hallway during the change of class and who runs up to another student, picks him up, and smashes him to the floor would most certainly be viewed as having a "problem." However, that same behavior performed in the gym during a wrestling competition would be praised and prized. In each case, the behavior is identified as adjusted (i.e., normal) or maladjusted as a function of the context within which it is applied.

From the behavioral frame of reference, behaviors are situation adaptive or maladaptive and the goal of a behavioral counselor would be to assist the student to be able to employ "adaptive" behaviors. For the counselor employing a behavioral perspective, it is not about moving a student from being sick to becoming well, or moving a pathological child back to normal. The emphasis that a school counselor with a behavioral orientation brings to counseling is that it is about learning what is functional and adaptive and assisting the student in their development and employment of these adaptive skills.

More Than Understanding . . . Controlling!

Now the word "controlling" often elicits images of an Orwellian type society where everyone moves about as an automaton—and all human spirit is lost—controlled by some "big brother." This is not the meaning of the word control, as used here and as reflective of a behavioral orientation.

Those school counselors working from a behavioral-orienting framework approach their work with the view of an experimenter. They envision their interventions as "treatment" in an experiment. As such, each intervention, each "experimental treatment" is grounded in data and firm rationale, and is assessed for impact.

The language of control is one that implies the causal connection between the intervention employed and the outcomes desired and achieved. Thus, the school counselor with a behavioral orienting framework seeks not only to understand the student's concern, and perhaps facilitate insight, but also to use this understanding to provide the means for "controlling" this behavior, and this situation.

While this language of control may, on first blush, be disconcerting to the school counselor, it must be remembered that it is not the control by another that is desired, but rather the ability to control the elements affecting undesirable and desired behaviors. Consider the simple illustration of a student who is seeking assistance with his dieting plan.

As the counselor and student engage in the process of defining the problem, identifying the goals, and then gathering data about current eating behaviors, they discover that a pattern of eating sweets prior to dinner seems to be adding unnecessary and undesired calories. In reviewing the data on this behavior, the counselor and student come to the following conclusions. First, the student is hungry having eaten lunch at 10:30 A.M. and now having to wait until 5:00 P.M. for dinner. Secondly, there are highly visible and easily accessible high-caloric snacks placed on the kitchen counter, which seem to "invite" the student's partaking. With these data, the counselor and student devise the following plan to "control" (i.e., reduce) this undesirable snaking. First, the student will put away all high-caloric snacks, placing them off the counter and into a pantry and thus making them less visible and less "inviting." Secondly, the student will place fresh fruit on the kitchen counter, a food that he enjoys, and he will have a prepared, low-calorie dip available in the refrigerator. The final adjustment implemented in an attempt to "control" this student's undesirable snacking behavior, is that the student will eat a 190 calorie low-carbohydrate, power bar during his ride home as a means of reducing his hunger urge.

In this simple illustration—*control* of the student's hunger urge and his self-identified undesirable snacking behavior are the targets. These are targets selected by the student *and* the student is the one empowered to gain control. The "researcher" mindset of the school counselor employing a behavioral perspective will result in additional data gathering in order to test the connection between the "treatment" and its impact (i.e., control) over the outcome. This is truly a mini-experiment, with systematic observations, the manipulation of variables, and outcomes recorded.

The "experiment nature" and focus on control is illustrated in the following exchange.

Student: I love the beach and the warmth of the sun. It's funny as I close my eyes, I can almost hear the ocean. Wow—this is so cool. It really is relaxing.

Counselor: Tina, you have wonderful ability to create images. Stay with it for a moment. See if you continue to feel relaxed.

(after a few moments)

Student: Unbelievable. This really works.

Counselor: How about if we try a mini-experiment. When you were rating your anxiety last week, you recorded that you were at a 7 or 8 anytime you knew you were the next to go up to the board to do some work, and you were at a 3 or 4 (less anxious) when you had to give the report to your small work group.

Student: Yeah?

Counselor: Well, how about if we start with the group reports. If I understood correctly, people go around the group and report on the research they did.

Student: Yes, and I'm usually the third one to go . . . since we always sit in the same places.

Counselor: Great. So how about, while the first two members are sharing their findings, you create that image of the beach that you have been using, simply close your eyes . . . breathing smoothly and rhythmically and capture that warmth of that image of the beach. Could you do that?

Student: Sure. See we have to pass out a written summary—so I could make it like I was looking down at the sheet.

Counselor: Okay. And I want you to observe how you feel when you start to speak. I am thinking that the breathing and the imaging may help you move down the scale even lower than the 3 or 4.

Student: But, what happens if I can't get the image back or stay on it when they are talking?

Counselor: Well, remember I said this was a mini-experiment. Whatever happens will be useful information and we can look at it and then adjust our plans in response to it. How's that sound?

Student: Sounds like a plan. Let's give it a try.

The counselor in the above scenario is not only inviting the student to approach the utilization of the intervention as a reflective researcher, but the goal of the intervention is one of control, that is, controlling the student's anxiety.

As will become evident in our discussion of intervention strategies, the techniques employed by the school counselor using a behavioral perspective are done with one purpose in mind—to help the student become more adaptive and effective in his or her functioning.

Behavioral Counseling: A Data-Driven Process

A final assumption and operative value embraced by counselors using a behavioral perspective is that counseling is a data-driven process. Those counselors employing a behavioral-orienting framework employ data as the bases for the development, implementation, maintenance, and evaluation of interventions. Operating from the previous assumptions, which suggest that all behavior is responsive to circumstances and is intended to be functional, the school counselor is interested in understanding the nature and context within which these behaviors occur. It is through the specific gathering of data that reveals the "what," "when," and even the implied "why" or to "what end" the behavior of concern occurs, leading the counselor and student to begin to see points of intervention emerging.

Consider the situation when a student is referred to the counseling office because he "refused to complete his deskwork." The counselor with a behavioral-orienting framework will want to more fully understand the context of this behavior. Following observation of the student within the classroom, the counselor may note that the student, who has severe ADHD, is seated next to a gerbil cage at the back of the classroom. Further, by collecting and analyzing data depicting time on task, the counselor hypothesized that that inattentiveness was due to the distraction of the visual and auditory stimulation coming from the gerbil on its exercise wheel.

Under these conditions, an intervention could be as simple as removing the stimulation and/or assisting the student to learn self-management strategies geared to reducing the impact of these distracting stimuli and "refocusing" on the deskwork. Contrast this to the situation when data reveal that the student's "refusal to complete the deskwork" resulted in the teacher approaching his desk, bending down to eye level, and spending up to two minutes encouraging the student to do his work. Further, assume that these data paint a picture that suggests that these are the only times this student receives such individualized and extensive teacher attention. In this context, the failure to complete deskwork appears to be a behavior that is in fact reinforced—supported—by way of teacher attentiveness. Certainly, under these conditions, the intervention employed will differ from that of our first scenario. Perhaps with the teacher's attention serving as the "payoff," the counselor may attempt to use that attention only when the student is on task, while withholding it when he is off task. The expectation is that changing the student's on-task behavior will increase in frequency now that it is the means to gain what is desired—teacher attention.

In both scenarios, it was the specific data depicting the events surrounding the occurrence of the behavior of concern that provided the direction for the development of the specific interventions. Behavioral counseling is data driven.

STEPS GUIDING A BEHAVIORALLY-ORIENTED COUNSELOR'S DECISIONS

The school counselor working from a behavioral-orienting framework approaches each encounter with students having embraced each of the previous operative assumptions. From this framework, the school counselor's reflections and decisions, while tailored to the uniqueness of each student, proceeds according to the following steps (see Figure 2.1).

Figure 2.1   Guiding Steps to Reflective Practice for a Behavioral-Orienting
Framework

Identify who is to be involved in assessment and intervention.

⇩

Identify the BORC (behavior of real concern).

⇩

Collect data for functional-behavioral analysis.

⇩

Analyze data for contract and set goals.

⇩

Develop/implement intervention strategies to facilitate change.

⇩

Monitor and adjust.

⇩

Plan for maintenance and relapse prevention.

Identifying Who Is Involved

While it may appear to be a rather simple question to ask—"who should be involved in assessment and intervention processes?"—it really is not as simple to answer. When using a behavioral approach, the door is open to include numerous people in varying roles. While the counselor and the student can certainly be active agents in assessing and intervening in the situation, it is not unusual for either the counselor, the student, or both to decide on the inclusion of significant others into the process, including teachers, parents, and even peers. It is quite possible that a counselor may choose to work directly with a teacher—in a consultation mode—in order to gather the data needed for assessment and even use the teacher as the implementer of the intervention. That same process could be used with parents, as well. It is also not outside of the model to have the student collect the needed assessment information and even employ or, if you will, apply the intervention strategy in a self-monitoring plan. So, a first step to treatment planning when operating from a behavioral orientation is to decide who will gather the assessment data, develop the interventions, and then implement.

Defining Behaviors of Real Concern (BORC)

During the initial session, the counselor operating from a behavioral-orienting framework will assist the student in defining his or her area of concern (behavior of real concern, BORC) in specific, concrete, and measurable terms.

A BORC constitutes a behavior that we do, or fail to do, that is causing us some real problem. For example, both the student who spends too much time going over her work, ruminating about possible mistakes, and, as a result, often stays up late into the night and experiences debilitating anxiety; and the student who is an overeater; exhibit what could be termed as "excess" BORCs. These behaviors are problematic in the fact of their excess; they are problems of commission. However, the student who fails to complete her homework, or who withdraws from all peer interaction, would be demonstrating deficit BORCs. These behaviors are problematic in their deficit or deficiency.

While these behaviors, as with all behavior, serve a purpose—a function—they become behaviors of real concern as a result of the consequences that follow. The student ruminating over her test performance may experience debilitating anxiety, and the student failing to complete homework assignments may encounter not only failing grades but also parental reprimands as a consequence. It is these undesirable consequences that define the behaviors as behaviors of real concern.

In order for the counselor and student to fully understand the factors that may be contributing to the creation and maintenance of a BORC, these behaviors of real concern need to be defined in concrete, observable terms. Thus, rather than simply stating that a student is aggressive, this aggression would need to be defined in observable, concrete terms as either verbal and/or physical, using descriptors pointing to "how it looks." In this illustration, the behavior of concern may be described as physically hitting other students during study hall. Similarly, rather than simply stating that a student is out of control and hyper, the school counselor would want to translate this BORC into the observable, concrete form such as, "The student calls out answers without raising his hand and waiting to be recognized," and/or, "The student leaves his seat without permission." Table 2.1 provides examples of this concretization of presenting concerns.

With the behavior of real concern defined in measurable terms, the counselor and student are now in the position to collect the data needed for the formulation of an effective intervention.

Table 2.1   Operationalizing BORCs

Presenting Concern	Operationalized Definition
Student is disruptive in class.	During class-challenge rounds, student calls out answers without first raising his hand and waiting to be recognized.
Student is mean.	During recess, student refuses to let other students join the game she is playing, and hits them on the head if they try to join in.
Student is hyperactive.	Student leaves seat without asking permission.
Student has a problem in class.	Student talks to peers and plays with cell phone in class.
Student has difficulty with anger.	Student physically punches and chokes other students when angry.
Student is self-destructive.	Student cuts self in the forearm and thigh.

Review of History and Context

An application of the "data" orientation embraced by school counselors with a behavioral orientation will lead much of the initial session(s) to focus on gathering information about the student's history with this situation, in hopes of unearthing antecedent stimuli that may be eliciting the behavior under consideration, as well as any consequential elements that may come into play in supporting the BORC. A secondary purpose of such history taking is to help the student begin to understand the learned nature of this behavior of concern. This insight provides the foundation for the development of a collaborative hope-filled relationship that will support the student's "learning" of more adaptive behaviors.

Data Collection for Functional Behavioral Assessment (FBA)

Once the behavior is clearly defined, the next step would be to gather data that will shed light on the possible elements supporting these behaviors. A functional assessment attempts to identify antecedent stimuli or circumstances that may serve to cue or elicit the behavior. Further, the assessment will investigate the immediate consequences following the behavior. The counselor is interested in identifying any possible events that may serve to strengthen the frequency and intensity of the behavior (i.e., reinforcement). The assessment is truly an in-depth attempt to answer the question, "What function does the behavior serve?"

By designing an intervention based on the function rather than the form of behavior, a number of benefits are obtained (Lane, Umbreit, & Beebe-Frankenberger, 1999). First, the emphasis is on skill building and supporting prosocial behavior, with less emphasis on punitive intervention strategies that simply seek to reduce behavior problems. Second, by using hypothesis-driven treatment, positive outcomes are more likely. Third, function-based interventions increase the likelihood that the new behavior(s) will produce meaningful, lasting change, which is the objective of all intervention efforts.

Once data are collected, function-based decisions can be made in an attempt to identify two pivotal questions: (a) "Is the desired behavior in the student's repertoire?" and (b) "Do the current classroom practices represent effective practices?"

A function-based intervention decision tree has been developed by Umbreit et al. (2004) and is reprinted in Figure 2.2.

Figure 2.2 Function-Based Intervention Decision Tree

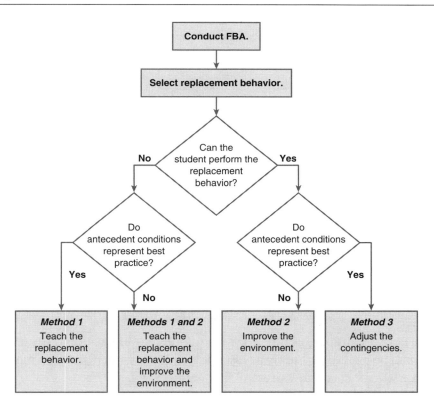

SOURCE: From Umbreit, John, et al. *Functional Behavioral Assessment and Function-Based Intervention*, 1e. Published by Allyn and Bacon/Merrill Education, Boston, MA. Copyright © 2006 by Pearson Education. Reprinted by permission of the publisher.

Table 2.2 provides some illustrations of the type of functions serviced by particular student behaviors. These are presented merely as illustrations and not intended to be an exhaustive listing.

Table 2.2   Common Function of Illustrative BORCs

Function Served	Sample BORCs
Gaining attention.	Entering class late, dramatic.
	Talking during "quiet time."
	Making noises.
	Responding to teacher in ways to elicit peer laughter.
	Dramatic crying, protesting etc.
Escaping or avoiding aversive situation.	Acting out and receiving "time-out" or class removal.
	Withdrawing from class participation as a means of avoiding board work.
	Throwing temper tantrum as means of being allowed to stay home rather than go to school.
	Acting out any behavior to get sent out of the class.
	Being "sick" as a means to avoid a test, presentation, or other anxiety provoking event.
Obtaining a desired object or experience.	Bullying to get a peer's "respect" or "lunch money."
	Giving the teacher attitude in order to push her button and watch her "lose it."
	Refusing to participate until given a position next to the teacher.
	Acting overwhelmed and helpless to elicit teacher or peer support in doing a particular task.
	Making a scene—crying, yelling; in general, melting down as a way to be first on the computer or play at the finger painting table.

There are numerous interview techniques or observational strategies that can be used to gather these essential data; one rather common model, an A-B-C log or record, is presented in Figure 2.3.

This record is merely a tool to record several occurrences of the BORC and any observed conditions preceding (antecedents) or following (consequences) that may appear connected.

Figure 2.3   A-B-C Log: Data Guiding Reflection "on" Practice

Student Name:		Observation Date:	
Observer:		Time:	
Activity:		Class Period:	
Behavior of concern (concretely, operationally defined):			
Antecedent		*Behavior*	*Consequence*

There are other observational tools and interview strategies that have been developed for the gathering of these data. Many of these strategies will be illustrated in the chapters that follow; however, an in-depth look at these approaches to functional assessment is well beyond the scope of this text. Readers interested in additional insight into these techniques should refer to the Resources listed at the end of the chapter.

Analyzing Data for Contract and Setting Goals

In looking for an answer to the question "what function does this BORC serve," the counselor and student will investigate the occurrence of recurring patterns associated with the behavior. Are there specific antecedent conditions that seem to elicit this behavior, or perhaps are there consequences that strengthen and support it? In answering this question, the school counselor and student will find directions for effective goal setting and intervention planning.

Consider the following two illustrations of a student who disrupts the class with his use of "poking." As you read the brief vignettes and review the data presented in the charts, begin to draw your own hypotheses about treatment options. Is the problem of "poking" the same in both cases? Will the same intervention strategy work for both students?

CASE 1: ANGELO

Angelo was referred to the counselor's office because, according to his teacher, "He cannot keep his hands to himself." In meeting with the teacher, the counselor discovered that this phrase was meant to convey the fact that Angelo often uses his index finger to poke the student sitting in front of him in the back. The teacher has talked to Angelo about this behavior and has given him detentions but nothing to date has worked. Working with the teacher, the following data were gathered (Table 2.3).

Table 2.3 Angelo's A-B-C Log

Student Name: Angelo	Observation Date: Nov 12, 2008	
Observer: J. Henderson	Time: 10 A.M. to 11 A.M.	
Activity: Doing deskwork, problem solving.	Class Period: third-period math (sixth grade)	
Behavior of concern (concretely, operationally defined): using a finger or writing instrument to push or poke the student seated directly in front him, in the back.		
Antecedent	*Behavior*	*Consequence*
Works on math problem. Throws down his pencil and places head in hands.	Pushes the student in the back.	Apologizes to the student and returns to desk work.
Attempts to finish prior to time expenditure. Teacher just called for papers.	Pokes the student with his finger, while throwing paper to the front.	Teacher reprimands, and sends Angelo out of the classroom.

CASE 2: WALLACE

Wallace, or as he prefers, Wally, was sent to the counselor's office because he has been "poking" students with his finger or pens and pencils, causing the students to become angry and often lash out. The teacher has employed time out, and punishment in the form of detention, but the behavior continues. Data were collected by the teacher and these are presented in the following table (Table 2.4).

Table 2.4   Wally's A-B-C Log

Student Name: Wally	Observation Date: Nov 12, 2008	
Observer: J. Henderson	Time: 10 A.M. to 11 A.M.	
Activity: Doing seatwork, problem solving.	Class Period: third-period math (sixth grade)	
Behavior of concern (concretely, operationally defined): using a finger or writing instrument to push, or poke the student seated directly in front of him, in the back.		
Antecedent	*Behavior*	*Consequence*
Works on math problem. Finishes before other students. Looks around the class and plays with his pencil.	Pushes the student in the back.	Students nearby laugh and Wally gives a thumbs-up sign.
Completes a packet of materials. Teacher announces the class has five more minutes to work on them before passing them forward.	Pokes the student with his finger—multiple times.	Student yells, "stop it." Teacher redirects class to finish their work and comes down to privately reprimand Wally. The "discussion" continues for approximately three minutes. Teacher returns to front of the class. Wally smiles.

As we review these very brief case presentations and limited data, it is clear that "poking" for both students involves pushing another student in the back with a finger or writing instrument. However, when investigating the antecedent conditions and consequences which appear associated with the occurrence of this behavior, are there any significant differences which may lead you, as counselor, to conclude that the behavior of poking serves a different function for each of these students, and thus a different form of intervention is required?

The counselor working with these two students would employ this data analyses to generate hypotheses about the function served by each BORC and therefore set a direction for both the establishment of achievable goals and the nature of an intervention. Figure 2.4 provides a schema of this process of data analyses.

Figure 2.4   Constructing Hypotheses

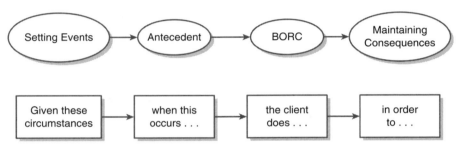

If we use Angelo as the test case, it could be concluded that, "When doing deskwork, when Angelo becomes frustrated, he pokes his classmate in order to release his frustration." This hypothesis is derived by viewing the observations through the lens provided in Figure 2.4. In this brief illustration, it appears that Angelo's behavior occurs when attempting to complete deskwork (Given these circumstances), and encountering task difficulty and frustration (When this occurs). With these as the antecedent conditions, Angelo engages in the BORC of poking his classmate (this is what the client does), which appears to serve as a release for his frustration (in order to . . .). While responding to these eliciting conditions (antecedents), Angelo gives evidence of understanding the inappropriateness of the behavior (e.g., offering immediate apologies).

However, Wally's behavior appears to increase during times of inactivity. His behaviors appear to be instrumental in gaining peer attention (consequences that follow the BORC). While his behaviors have resulted in teacher reprimands, it appears that this attention also is more desirable than the absence of stimulation he encounters during these down periods. Thus, his poking behaviors serve the function of gaining desired attention.

Developing/Implementing Strategies for Intervention

By analyzing the data, the counselor will be able to develop intervention plans and strategies that will facilitate the student's ability to behave in more appropriate and adaptive ways. The goal is not to merely stop the student from being "bad," but rather to help that student to develop the strategies, the behaviors, which allow him or her to function and succeed in this school environment.

While the specifics of the intervention plan will be tailored to the individual student—the BORC—and the data gathered from the analyses of antecedents and consequences, generally the interventions will target:

1. Modification and manipulation of the antecedents and/or consequences associated with the behavior.

2. Alternative response training that helps the student achieve the same purpose and function (e.g., attention seeking), but through more adaptive behavior.

3. Modification of physical and learning environments (including curriculum) as a way of eliciting desired behavior.

Specific intervention strategies are discussed in depth in the remainder of this book. But, as a simple illustration of the value of data analyzes to intervention planning, let's return to Angelo and Wally—two pokers.

Assuming that the conclusions drawn from these data are accurate, the school counselor may attempt to address Angelo's "poking" by reducing the frustrating stimuli (i.e., change curriculum), and/or providing Angelo with alternative response training (e.g., relaxation training) to be used during periods of frustration and failure. However, this same counselor may attempt to reduce Wally's "poking" by eliminating the attention he gains from this behavior and, in its place, arrange for teacher and peer attention to be contingent on his willingness to help other students or to assist the teacher during these periods of inactivity.

Monitoring and Adjusting Interventions

Even when interventions are developed based on the data acquired through the functional assessment, they will often need fine-tuning and adjustment as the student and counselor attempt to move the concept of intervention to the practice of intervening. It is important for the counselor to help the student embrace a researcher's mindset and approach each application of an intervention as a "mini-experiment," one where the strategy is employed, data reflecting the impact is gathered, and in subsequent sessions, strategies are adjusted. This monitoring and ongoing adjustment of intervention strategies (reflection "on" practice) serves as the focus for subsequent sessions.

Planning for Maintenance and Relapse Prevention

As the student and counselor move toward termination, a major focus of the reflection "on" practice will be on the identification of strategies that will help the student maintain his or her new behavior(s) as he or she moves back to the normal rhythm of his or her life. It is not unusual for the student to experience a reappearance of the BORC. Setbacks may be the result of the student and counselor failing to identify specific conditions that may continue to exist that would be challenges to the student in his or her efforts to maintain the new behavior. For example, while Lillian (age 8) has worked really hard on developing new eating behaviors and avoiding sweets, she experienced a significant setback, during her "Camp Fire" girls' outing. Neither the counselor nor Lillian anticipated the presence of sweets or the ongoing encouragement for eating sweets (i.e., the making and eating of "s'mores"—melted chocolate, marshmallow, and graham cracker) that would take place over her week camping adventure. If this trip had been discussed in session, Lillian and the counselor could have identified strategies that may have helped reduce the likelihood of the relapse, including developing strategies to avoid or resist eating the sweets and/or planning on taking acceptable treats that could have been used as substitutes for the s'mores.

Just as it was essential to analyze the antecedent conditions and consequences of the BORC when formulating an intervention, it is important to reconsider these factors as they may contribute to the maintenance of the client's gains as well as to help prevent relapse. As was the situation with Lillian, the reintroduction of the antecedent conditions (i.e., presence of sweets) can elicit the undesired behavior, but so may the failure to plan for ongoing reinforcement of the new behavior result in a return of the BORC.

It is important that the counselor assist the student in incorporating everyday rewards into the program as a way of maintaining the desired response. Therefore, while a student may have been earning points for learning to raise her hand before calling out a response in class, now as the use of these points is reduced, other rewards such as teacher praise, or even self-affirmation (e.g., "I'm doing great!"), need to be employed.

PUTTING IT TOGETHER

Prior to moving on to our discussion of specific interventions and the illustration of their applications, we close this chapter with a case illustrating the phases of a behavioral paradigm as applied to a problem with homework completion (Case Illustration 2.1).

Case Illustration 2.1   Akia—Homework Completion

Akia is a sixth-grade student whose grades are declining as a result of her failure to complete home assignments.

Step 1: Identify who is to be involved in assessment and intervention.

During the initial encounter, in addition to developing a comfortable working relationship with the student, the counselor explored the possibility of enlisting her teachers and her mother in the counseling process.

Counselor: Akia, I truly appreciate your openness and willingness to talk with me. Do you have any idea why I wanted to see you?

Akia: Yeah . . . 'cause I'm failing.

Counselor: Well (looking at current grades), actually, you are not failing. But your teachers are reporting that you are not handing in your homework.

Akia: I know. I keep saying that I need to do my homework and I know I can, but then I get home and I don't know what happens. I just don't think about homework until the next morning, and then it's too late.

Counselor: Akia, have you always had difficulty completing your homework and home assignments? Did you have difficulty last year?

Akia: We didn't get a lot of homework at Penn Woods Elementary. The teachers give a lot of work here.

Counselor: Well, I guess it is a bit different in middle school.

Akia: I've never failed (starting to tear up), and my mom's going to be really angry.

Counselor: I can see it is upsetting—but remember, we still have some time to turn things around. Do you think that maybe you and I could look at what's going on and figure out what to do?

Akia: I guess. But I don't want you to tell my mom.

In reflecting "on" practice, the counselor recognizes the student's need and interest to approach this as a self-management process, and until and unless it becomes clear that the involvement of others is needed or of value, the counselor is willing to proceed just with the student.

Counselor: Well, how about for now, you and I attack it, but I would like to talk to your teachers in order to find out exactly what it is they would like to see happen. Is that okay?

Akia: Okay.

(Continued)

(Continued)

Step 2: Identify the BORC (behavior of real concern).

While Akia initially presented the "problem" as her failing, this "problem" was re-defined in more specific, concrete terms as "not completing homework assignments." However, prior to engaging in data collection, the counselor wants to be clear about the actual goal and, as such, needs to engage Akia in order to define the goal of choice.

Counselor:	Akia, it appears that you are not doing your homework, and that's the thing we want to work on.
Akia:	It's not all my homework. I always do my English homework. It's really just my math homework I don't do.
Counselor:	So, you do your English homework. What type of homework do you typically have for English class?
Akia:	It's always vocabulary. We have a list of words that we have to use in sentences. I like writing. I always try to use the new words in my diary and when I am IM-ing my friends.
Counselor:	IM-ing?
Akia:	Instant messaging (smiling).
Counselor:	Okay you got me . . . I'm old. But that's really cool. You actually use the words with friends. Okay, so English isn't problem; you really like working with the vocabulary. But, hmmm, math is another issue.
Akia:	Yeah. I understand it and get good test grades. I just don't like doing the problems.
Counselor:	Okay, how would you feel if we could figure out a way that you not only would do your math homework, but actually even enjoy doing it?
Akia:	That would be great. I don't like failing (starting to tear up).
Counselor:	Well, I think we are already taking some steps to get you where you want to go. I mean, you are here and you have helped to identify what exactly it is that we want to work on—math homework. Now, I'm going to need your help. Okay?
Akia:	What do I have to do?
Counselor:	Don't worry (smiling). It's not painful. I need you to do some detective work for me.

Step 3: Collect data for functional-behavioral analysis.

Counselor:	Akia, you said that you keep a diary and you use your new vocabulary words when you write in it. I'm wondering, would you keep another kind of diary for me?

Akia:	A diary?
Counselor:	Well not a diary . . . more like a scientist's journal or log.
Akia:	I'm not sure what you mean.
Counselor:	Okay. Here's what I'm asking you to do. You said you have vocabulary homework every night. How often do you have math problems to do?
Akia:	Every night.
Counselor:	Okay. So, here's what I want you to do. I would like you to write in this "journal" (handing Akia a small copy book), the following things (writing down instructions on the first page).

Homework Log

Day: write down the day of the week.

Time: write down what time you start.

Place: describe where you are doing your homework.

What's going on: describe, and you can use your new vocabulary if you want, what is going on right before you begin your homework. (For example, maybe you were playing, or watching television, or helping your mom or IM-ing your friends.) Write as much as you can about what's going on and what you are doing prior to doing your homework.

What you are doing: describe what you did. (For example, "I worked ten minutes on vocabulary" or "I did four math problems.")

What happened afterwards: decribe what you did, what happened, if anything, to you, how you felt . . . right after you stopped during your homework.

Counselor:	Now, I know that's a lot, but do you think you could do that?
Akia:	I like doing science stuff, so I'm sure it will be fine—but what happens if I don't do the homework? You know, I forget?
Counselor:	Well, that's something we want to look at. I promise you, no lecture from me. We'll just look at what was going on and see if we can figure out how to use this information to help you do your homework. Okay?

Step 4: Analyze data for contract and set goals.

Following three days of data collection, Akia and the counselor met. The counselor's reflections resulted in setting the following goals for the upcoming session: (1) invite Akia to share on her experience and anything else she wants to share; (2) affirm the value of her data collection and her willingness to be actively involved; (3) review the data in order to establish reasonable goals; and (4) begin to identify targets for manipulation. The exchange that follows picks up in midsession.

(Continued)

(Continued)

Counselor:	Okay, so it looks like after we talked, you did all of your homework. That's great. And, it looks like on Wednesday and Thursday you did your vocabulary homework—wow, you worked for thirty minutes each night on vocabulary. It looks like after you did your vocabulary, you got a snack and went online with your friends. Akia, you have fantastic notes here.
Akia:	Thanks!
Counselor:	It looks like you are really good about starting your homework right after you come home from school. All three days you started by 3:30.
Akia:	Yeah . . . my mom wants me to have it finished before dinner.
Counselor:	How does your mom feel about you going online with your friends?
Akia:	She's okay with it . . . but just until dinnertime. After dinner it's family time, no computer.
Counselor:	Family time? That's really nice. Akia, I'm wondering what happens if you have a lot of homework and you are busy with it all the way up to dinner? What happens to computer time?
Akia:	Nothing—I just don't get online that night.
Counselor:	So, in some way it seems that the less time you spend on homework, the more time you can have on the computer?
Akia:	Yeah, I guess.
Counselor:	So, if we could figure out a way you could do all of your homework and still have computer time—that may be a good thing?
Akia:	Yeah.
Counselor:	Okay, so could you keep collecting information for the next couple of days, but this time, maybe we could try one little change.
Akia:	What change?
Counselor:	What do you think would happen if you made a deal with yourself where you agreed to do your vocabulary work *and* one math problem *before* you go on the computer?
Akia	I could do that. I could do more than one.
Counselor:	Well, that would be super. But how about if we set as a goal at least one math homework problem before IM-ing your friends.

Step 5: Develop/implement intervention strategies to facilitate change.

The mini-experiment of doing one math homework problem prior to getting online is being used as a test to see if being online could be used as a payoff for doing homework. If this seems to be the case, then plans would be developed to make going online contingent upon completing all homework.

Step 6: Monitor and adjust.

In subsequent sessions, the counselor and Akia would expand the requirement from doing a couple of homework problems prior to going online to eventually being required to complete all homework problems prior to going online. If the data reveal that completing all her homework required Akia to use all her after school time for homework, the counselor and Akia may consider asking Akia's mother to allow Akia to go online after dinner, if she has completed all homework.

Step 7: Plan for maintenance and relapse prevention.

Assuming Akia achieved her goals of completing all mathematics homework, the counselor would help Akia identify the benefits of her new homework behavior. It is hoped that the "natural" payoffs of improved grades, increased positive feedback from teachers and the reduction of her own stress and concern about her mother finding out would serve to maintain this behavior.

SUMMARY

Counseling with a behavioral perspective engages the school counselor in the systematic utilization of observational data and the employment of the scientific method in the development, implementation, and assessment of his or her interventions.

Behaviorism As Naturalistic

- A fundamental assumption undergirding a behavioral orientation is that everything, including all human behavior, can be explained in terms of natural laws.

Behavior Acquired Through Conditioning

- Behaviorists, while embracing the influence of genetics, value and highlight the impact of experience—learning—conditioning in the shaping of our human behavior.

(Continued)

(Continued)

Dysfunctional Behavior Rather Than Pathological Individuals

- From the behavioral frame of reference, behaviors are situation adaptive or maladaptive and the goal of a behavioral counselor would be to assist the student to be able to employ "adaptive" behaviors.

More Than Understanding . . . Controlling!

- The school counselor with a behavioral-orienting framework seeks not only to understand the student's concern, and perhaps facilitate insight, but also to use this understanding to provide the means for "controlling" this behavior, and this situation.

Behavioral Counseling: A Data Driven Process

- Counselors employing a behavioral-orienting framework employ data as the bases for the development, implementation, maintenance, and evaluation of interventions.

STEPS GUIDING A BEHAVIORALLY-ORIENTED COUNSELOR'S DECISIONS

Identifying Who Is Involved

- When using a behavioral approach, the door is open to include numerous people in varying roles. While the counselor and the student can certainly be active agents in assessing and intervening in the situation, it is not unusual for either the counselor, the student, or both to decide on the inclusion of significant others into the process, including teachers, parents, even peers.

Defining Behaviors of Real Concern (BORC)

- During the initial session, the counselor operating from a behavioral-orienting framework will assist the student in defining his or her area of concern (behavior of real concern, BORC) in specific, concrete, and measurable terms.
- A BORC constitutes a behavior that we do, or fail to do, that is causing us some real problem.

Reviewing History and Context

- An application of the "data" orientation embraced by school counselors with a behavioral orientation will lead much of the initial session(s) to focus on gathering information about the student's history with this situation, in hopes of unearthing antecedent stimuli that may be eliciting the behavior under consideration, as well as any consequential elements that may come into play in supporting the BORC.

Data Collection: Functional Behavioral Assessment (FBA)

- A functional assessment attempts to identify antecedent stimuli or circumstances that may serve to cue or elicit the behavior. Further, the assessment will investigate the immediate consequences following the behavior.

Analyzing Data for Contract and Goal Setting

- In looking for an answer to the question "what function does this BORC serve" the counselor and student will investigate the occurrence of recurring patterns associated with the behavior. Are there specific antecedent conditions that seem to elicit this behavior or perhaps are there consequences that strengthen and support it? In answering this question, the school counselor and student will find directions for effective goal setting and intervention planning.

Developing/Implementing Strategies for Intervention

- The goal is not to merely stop the student from being "bad," but rather to help that student to develop the strategies, the behaviors, which allow him or her to function and succeed in this school environment.
- Interventions typically target:
  1. Modification and manipulation of the antecedents and/or consequences associated with the behavior.
  2. Alternative response training that helps the student achieve the same purpose and function (e.g., attention seeking), but through more adaptive behavior.
  3. Modification of physical and learning environments (including curriculum) as a way of eliciting desired behavior.

(Continued)

(Continued)

Monitoring and Adjusting Interventions

- Interventions are developed based on the data acquired through the functional assessment. They will often need fine-tuning and adjustment as the student and counselor attempt to move the concept of intervention to the practice of intervening. This monitoring and ongoing adjustment of intervention strategies (reflection "on" practice) serves as the focus for subsequent sessions.

Planning for Maintenance and Relapse Prevention

- As the student and counselor move toward termination, a major focus of the reflection "on" practice will be on the identification of strategies that will help the student maintain his or her new behavior(s) as he or she moves back to the normal rhythm of his or her life.

Part II

Interventions Targeting the Increase, Decrease, and Substitution of Behavior

As is evident in the previous discussion, the school counselor employing a behavioral orientation to guide his or her reflective practice will rely on the development of clear, concrete goals, and functional behavioral assessment to guide selection of intervention strategy. The chapters found within Part II highlight the application of the behavioral framework to the creation, application, and maintenance of interventions which target (1) the increase of specific behavior(s) (Chapter 3), (2) the decrease of undesirable behavior(s) (Chapter 4), and (3) the creation of alternative response to eliciting stimuli (Chapter 5).

While each chapter assists the reader in understanding the rationale and steps to be taken while employing these interventions, the real value is in the detailed case illustrations that provide a view of the "mindset" of a school counselor operating with a behavioral-orienting framework. As you review the development and employment of each of the techniques, you will discover that the work of a school counselor operating from a behavioral orientation is focused, active, and directive. While continuing to employ those techniques core to all counseling, including summarizations, reflections and purposeful questioning, the behaviorally-oriented school counselor continually (1) directs the student to increased clarity and specification of goals; (2) employs functional behavior assessment to guide reflection and planning, allowing these data to give form to the interventions employed; and (3) embraces his or her role as a reflective-research practitioner providing problem-solving service.

As with all techniques described in counseling books such as this, the interventions presented gain value by way of the masterful timing and application at the hands of the effective school counselor. Just as a child may be able to make a sound with a simple slide whistle, in the hands of a musician this simple instrument can produce beautiful music. The same is true for the discourse and strategies employed in behaviorally oriented school counseling. With practice, supervisory feedback and engagement in reflection "on" and "in" practice, these techniques move from being simply paper narratives to becoming valuable tools within your own repertoire of counseling strategies.

Strategies Targeting **3** the Development of Behavior

Reward and punishment systems have been used throughout recorded history in an attempt to modify behavior. The successful employment of contingency management as a behavioral-modification process has been documented with use for a variety of populations and targeted behaviors (Kazdin, 2001). Contingency contracting and the use of rewards have proved effective for a variety of school-based problems, including reducing classroom tantrums (Wilkinson, 2003); improving academic achievement (Kelly & Stokes, 1984) and compliance (Olmi, Sevier, & Nastasi, 1997); and increasing homework completion rates (Bryan & Sullivan-Brustein, 1998), to name a few.

While the current chapter will provide detailed illustrations of the successful employment of operant conditioning techniques as interventions for increasing the frequency of desired behaviors, the scope and nature of this text prevents a detailed and elaborate explication of the subtleties of this method. Readers interested in detailed presentation of this approach should consult texts such as Kazdin (2001), Martin and Pear (2003), and Miltenberger (2004).

BEHAVIORAL DEFICIT

Quite often, the student presenting at our office does so with deficit or deficiency in terms of his or her behavioral options. The student failing math may be struggling because of the infrequency and/or inconsistency with which he engages in appropriate study and class preparation behaviors. Similarly, the student who seems reluctant to participate in class discussion may be giving evidence of a limited social skill set. Even the second-grade student referred to the counselor's office because of his "bullying" behavior, may in fact be illustrating his limited repertoire of cooperative behavior or social negotiations skills. The school counselor operating with a behavioral perspective understands that for each of these students, the target for counseling would be the development of a more appropriate, adaptable behavior. The intervention of choice would be the systematic employment of reinforcement to develop and maintain the desired behaviors.

The process certainly seems rather simple and straightforward. However, this is not the case. For many people untrained in behavioral strategies, the concepts of rewards and punishment seem quite simple and clear cut. For example, providing a candy to a child is a reward and similarly, hollering at the child or in some way providing negative feedback is most certainly a punishment. Well . . . not quite!

It is often the misunderstanding of behavioral principles and the unsystematic approach to using operant strategies taken by some school counselors that lead to their failures.

PROGRAMMING FOR GROWTH

The degree to which the employment of operant techniques is successful is to a large extent a function of the counselor's ability to use data to guide his or her systematic application of behavioral principles. Starting with the identification of the specific behavior to be increased, and proceeding through the employment of strategies targeting the maintenance of these newly acquired and desired behaviors, the counselor and student will gather, analyze, and employ data on behavioral change as the bases for all reflective practice. It is this "scientific," data-driven approach to creating, implementing, and evaluating interventions that serve as the hallmark of a behavioral approach to counseling.

While respecting the uniqueness of each student and student concern, the counselor operating from a behavioral perspective will frame his or her reflections and planning using the following targets as guidelines.

Selecting a Behavior for Modification

In Chapter 2, the importance of identifying behaviors of real concern and the concrete—operational—defining of desired goals was highlighted. The school counselor working with a behavioral orientation understands that it is only in specifying the desired behavior in concrete, measurable terms that one can be assured that the reinforcement program can be applied consistently and that real change can be noted.

Consider the case of a first-grade student, Emile, who was referred to the counselor because he was "simply out of control." While the teacher's referral highlighted some form of difficulty with Emile's behavior, the counselor knew that a more specific and concrete articulation of "out of control" was needed. Follow-up with the teacher presented the following scenario as concrete illustrations of Emile's behaviors of real concern.

- "Emile would run out of the classroom and hide—often under furniture or in unoccupied offices or bathrooms."
- When asked to attend to his work, Emile would resist and in a loud voice respond to the teacher, "Leave me alone!"

The goals identified were:

- To have Emile sit and perform independent deskwork when assigned.
- To have Emile raise his hand and wait to be recognized before asking a question or making a statement.
- To have Emile follow specific instructions to "line-up quietly," "sit on the carpet," and "clear the desk" without delay or protest.

Using Shaping

The use of reinforcement as an intervention for increasing the frequency of a desired behavior is an effective strategy, assuming that the desired behavior occurs at least occasionally. So, if we assume that Emile exhibited some of the desired behaviors and that the teacher would be able to provide reinforcement for these behaviors, then we could assume that an intervention plan would be relatively straightforward. However, what does the counselor, or the teacher, do if Emile fails to perform these actions and thus provides no opportunity for teacher or counselor reinforcement?

There are circumstances when the desired behavior is truly absent from the student's repertoire and thus will not be manifested. In situations when the student fails to exhibit the desired behavior, *shaping* may be employed as a procedure for developing a new behavior.

Shaping, also known as the method of successive approximations, can be defined as the gradual modification of a behavior reinforcing successive approximations of the desired behavior. Many of the behaviors we employ in our everyday functioning have been developed through the process of shaping.

Whether it be successfully driving a car, hitting a golf ball, or making a free throw in basketball, these refined behaviors generally start with very general, ill-refined movement—movement that slowly takes a final form as each adjustment results in a desired consequence. For those having had the experience of "teaching" someone to drive a stick-shift car, the process of shaping is all too painfully clear. Moving from popping the clutch and stalling, the student eventually shapes or molds the behavior of releasing the clutch so that smooth transition occurs.

A simple illustration of the process and value of shaping can be found in a situation working with a student who has fallen into the habit of not doing her homework. In this case, the counselor may be frustrated by the inability to reinforce homework behavior, since the student fails to give occasion that would allow such reinforcement. Under these conditions, shaping may prove more useful. Shaping allows the counselor and student to build the desired behavior in steps, and reward those behaviors that come progressively closer to the one identified as the terminal goal. As the student masters each step, they are required to move to the next increment in order to receive the reinforcement. For example, Ryan, an eighth-grade student, was referred because of her risk of failing in mathematics. Ryan's baseline data reveal that while she does well (90 percent average) on her tests, she is failing the class because she does not complete any of her mathematics homework assignments. Ryan expressed a desire to pass her class but reported that she hated to do the "stupid math problems" at home. With these data as the reference point and in consult with Ryan, an initial goal of completing two of the twenty problems was set as target. The counselor and Ryan established a "contract" that Ryan would earn Internet time, something she enjoyed, only if she successfully and neatly completed two of the assigned problems. In this situation, the "cost" (i.e., completing two homework problems) was less than the payoff (Internet time) and thus Ryan was willing and able to engage in this process. With success and contingent reinforcement, this target was increased sequentially to the point where all twenty problems assigned needed to be completed correctly in order to receive the reinforcement of going online.

Shaping is a very useful process, especially in situations where the counselor attempts to develop a behavior that never occurs or occurs with very low frequency. The following principles can be used to guide the counselor's reflective practice as she employs shaping as a process for developing a new behavior.

Defining Terminal Behavior to Starting Point

While it may appear somewhat backward, the first step is to concretely define the terminal or final behavior that is desired. As previously noted, this behavior needs to be defined in very specific, observable, and measurable terms. Thus, for our homework-resistant student, Ryan, the desired outcome might be for her to "accurately and neatly complete 100 percent of the assigned mathematics homework."

Establishing Subgoals

Once the terminal behavior is established and data depicting the student's current level of performance is reviewed, smaller, sequential subgoals can be identified and used as successive approximations, which will be reinforced. Thus, for Ryan, her first subgoal or approximation may be to accurately complete 20 percent of the assigned homework. As she demonstrates the ability to achieve this goal and experience the reinforcement contingent on the successful completion of that goal, the goal will be expanded to the next target. This sequential movement through the subgoals toward the approximated terminal goal is the process of shaping.

In our illustration, the terminal behavior was identified using a percentage of completion (100 percent). Thus, the steps that could be used in the shaping process could be as small as increasing in 1 percent increments. Selecting the size of these increments requires some good intuition and continued observation.

It is clear that when the terminal task appears to the student to be very difficult or even aversive, small steps will be needed. In contrast, for situations when the student has demonstrated a successful history with the terminal behavior, but who has more recently failed to manifest the desired terminal behavior, larger and thus less incremental steps may be the choice. In either case, it is important for the counselor and student to recognize that what is desired is for the student to be successful and to receive reinforcement, while moving through the successive approximations as quickly as possible.

Steadying Progress Towards Goal

When moving through the successive approximations, it is important to proceed toward the terminal goal using small enough steps to sufficiently make the "extra" effort, or cost, less than the accrued benefit of the reinforcement.

If it were possible for us to measure the unit of costs and payoff, we might find that Ryan doing one mathematics homework problem "costs" her a unit of discomfort, whereas the reinforcement employed provides her with three units of payoff. Under these conditions, we may be able to have her complete two or three homework problems in order to receive reinforcement. The costs required would be less than the payoff received.

The difficulty is that there is no such absolute measure of unit of cost or payoff. Thus, the counselor and student would have to make their best guess in terms of the size and number of steps, hoping to establish the least number of steps that would still insure steady progress toward the terminal goal. If, however, the behavior is lost as a result of moving too quickly or perhaps employing too large of a step, the counselor needs to return to the last successful approximation and redefine the subsequent steps.

Selecting Reinforcers

While it is intuitively appealing to state that things such as candy, stickers, good grades, and special attention are "rewards" for students, the truth is we only know a reward—a reinforcement—by the way it acts. This is a very important concept. A reinforcement is only a reinforcement *if* it strengthens the behavior that led to its reception.

A reinforcement truly is identified by how it operates. It is anything presented immediately following a specific behavior resulting in the increased likelihood and/or frequency of that behavior occurring. Thus, it is not whether you or I think something is desirable. The critical defining element to what constitutes a reinforcement is if that particular item results in increased frequency or probability of the behavior that led to its occurrence. This is a simple tenet, yet one which is easily confused and/or ignored.

Consider the situation where a teacher complains that one of her students, Lamar, seems totally out of control, regardless of what she, the teacher, has done. As the counselor investigates the situation, she gathers the following observations.

Antecedent	Behavior	Consequence
Students work in cooperative groups, teacher floats about the various groups to supervise work. Lamar sits in isolation with deskwork. Teacher begins to interact with a group at the front of the class.	Lamar drops his books on the floor with loud bang.	Teacher turns and "reprimands" Lamar, stating, "Lamar, please do your deskwork."

Antecedent	Behavior	Consequence
Lamar smiles, returns to working on deskwork. Teacher moves to a second group.	Lamar lets out a loud belch type sound.	Students laugh and teacher walks over to Lamar and warns him, "If you continue doing this I will have to send you down to Mrs. Morton" (assistant principal).
Lamar looks down and begins to do work. Teacher walks away and begins reviewing work done by group 3.	Lamar lets out a yell, "Ouch!" He looks at his middle finger, shaking it as if he pinched it.	Teacher yells, "That's it . . . take your books and get out of here. Go see Mrs. Morton and tell her you are not mature enough to be in sixth grade."

While one might feel that the various reprimands employed by the teacher would be more than noxious and something most students would want to avoid, it is clear that each one appeared to strengthen the various attention-getting behaviors employed by Lamar. In this situation, the teacher's "reprimands" actually served to increase the behavior which led to their employment, and thus by definition, these teacher actions were reinforcers!

We could speculate that perhaps Lamar desired attention, in any form, rather than the isolation he encountered. Or perhaps, Lamar found it satisfying to have evidence that he was controlling the situation and pushing the teacher's "buttons." The specific motivation is less important than understanding the reality that this teacher's attention given to Lamar following his disruptive behaviors actually served as reinforcement increasing the behavior that she hoped to decrease. Helping this teacher understand the concept of reinforcement and then learning how to systematically and differentially use her attention, to reinforce and promote the desired behavior, would be the focus for the school counselor.

So, an important principle to remember in identifying a reinforcer is that the event—or experience—must be experienced as desirable ("pleasant") by the individual for whom the reinforcement is intended. What may be a reinforcer, which is a pleasant experience for one student, need not be a reinforcer for another. In fact, it is not unusual to find that something that reinforced one student may actually be aversive or undesired by another. Consider the child in class who desires, even craves, teacher attention. There is a good chance that a word of praise or some teacher behavior that draws attention to this child will be received as a pleasant experience. However, the same teacher behavior that draws attention to a child who is socially anxious may be experienced as something painful and something to be escaped or avoided.

In identifying reinforcers, the counselor should look for events, conditions, and experiences that are pleasant to the student. For example, one group of reinforcers, called positive reinforcement, occurs when something pleasant is added (+) into the student's existence. Positive reinforcers can be categorized as: consumables (e.g., candy); activities (e.g., going to the mall); manipulatives (e.g., playing a video game); possessions (e.g., a new possession such as a CD); or social (e.g., receiving praise, hugs, or special attention). Consider the teacher working with Jeremy. The teacher has been trying to increase Jeremy's on-task behavior, and when she notices that Jeremy has opened his book and has begun to read as instructed she states, "Jeremy, I am really proud of you and the way you get right to work!" Assuming Jeremy finds these words of praise pleasant, their addition into the circumstance will increase his on-task behavior, thus identifying them as positive reinforcement. Pleasant events can also be experienced as a result of something seen as undesirable or noxious being removed from our experience. This second form of reinforcement, called negative reinforcement (−), occurs when a student discovers that something unpleasant or aversive has been removed following his or her engagement in a specific behavior.

In considering the illustration with Jeremy and the desire to increase his on-task behavior, another teacher chooses to walk over to Jeremy and with arms crossed and to engage in quiet staring at Jeremy as he plays and attempts to distract his peers. If Jeremy experiences this teacher's attention as uncomfortable and discovers that if he begins to read the assignment (rather than attempt to talk with his classmates), the teacher stops staring and walks away, he may employ this on-task behavior with greater frequency. If this removal of the teacher's stare results in Jeremy's increased on-task behavior, then the increase would have been the result of negative reinforcement (i.e., removal of an aversive experience). In this case, since it is by taking away or removing the event, the desired behavior is strengthened.

When possible, it is important to have the student identify things which he or she feels would work as reinforcement. One simple process would be to provide the student with a list of sample reinforcers as a starting point for this discussion. This point will be illustrated later in the chapter (see Case Illustration 3.2).

In Reinforcement, Size Does Matter

Reinforcement works because the student has a desire, a need for that which has been identified as a reinforcer. Because the student has been deprived of this particular event, the amount or magnitude of the reinforcer needs to be such to reduce this need or state of deprivation without totally satiating that need. For example, consider the case of a teen who was hoping to purchase an article of clothing costing $20.00. Assume that her parents suggested they would "pay" her for house cleaning but that the reception of the money was contingent on her performing these house cleaning duties. If that teen dusted and vacuumed one of the rooms in her house, and for her effort received $0.25, there is a really good chance that this would be the last time she voluntarily performed that act. Simply stated, the size of the "payoff" was too little to be a need satisfier and thus did not serve as reinforcement. Similarly, if that same teen dusted and vacuumed one room and received $20.00 for her efforts, the chance of her continuing in her cleaning duties and reaching the desired terminal goal, cleaning the house, may similarly be lessened. In this case, the amount of the initial reinforcement was so large as to totally satisfy the student's need. Since her need—having enough money to buy the article of clothing she desired—is satiated, her house-cleaning behavior will no longer be emitted.

As the counselor reflects "on" practice, she will need to monitor the ongoing need-satisfying value of the reinforcers employed.

Immediacy and Contingency

Since, by definition, reinforcement is what increases the frequency or intensity of the behavior that led to it, it is essential to close the time gap between the performance of the behavior and the reception of the reinforcement.

Consider the situation where the student who has been resistant doing deskwork completes the assignment in anticipation of receiving a word of praise or special attention from the teacher. However, the teacher is distracted and not immediately responsive. As the student sits waiting for the anticipated reward, time passes and he becomes frustrated. In this state of frustration, he starts to move in his chair and make subguttural noises. If now the teacher turns and praises him for the successful completion of his work, there is a chance that the behavior most immediately preceding the reception of the reinforcement—moving in the chair and noise making—may in fact be strengthened. One may wonder what behavior will increase in frequency, the deskwork, the movement and noise making, or perhaps a tandem response of deskwork and noise making? For maximum effectiveness, the reinforcer needs to be given immediately following the desired behavior (Martin & Pear, 2003).

Just as immediacy is an important factor in the distribution of reinforcement, so too it is important to ensure that the distribution is contingent on the performance of the target behavior. It is important to remember that reinforcement needs to be made contingent on the performance of the target behavior. Do *not* give reinforcement because you feel sorry for a student. If a student does not achieve the required criterion, delivering reinforcement will only teach the student that rewards are readily available regardless of behavior. Rather, in situations where the student is having difficulty performing the target behavior, the counselor can convey his or her awareness that the student is disappointed, while at the same time encouraging the student to try again. If the failure to achieve criterion continues, then the counselor should consider revisiting the subgoals, and when necessary, adjust the steps in the shaping process.

Employing "Natural" Reinforcers

Once the desired behavior has been developed and strengthened through the systematic application of operant reinforcement, the counselor needs to plan for the maintenance of this behavior once the "intervention program" is terminated. If we revisit our student who has been improving in her homework productivity because doing homework has earned her time online (Internet), the goal would be for this same student to perform her homework and receive the "payoffs" natural or more typical to the school setting. For many students, homework is completed because it results in higher grades, or in the ability to participate in class, or a personal sense of accomplishment. For these students, these experiences are received as pleasurable and contingent on successful homework achievement, and thus act as reinforcement. So, while we may employ reinforcers such as edibles (candy), or privilege (going online) to create the desired behavior, we want these behaviors to be maintained by the consequences typically encountered in the natural environment.

In this situation, the counselor identifies contingencies in the natural environment and then makes sure the terminal behavior is trapped (i.e., maintained) by these consequences. Thus, if we have helped a student increase his willingness to volunteer to do board work by using candy as a reinforcement, once this behavior appears established, we would want to begin to reduce the frequency with which the student is given candy, but in its place, the student would receive words of praise from the teacher and an awareness of a personal sense of achievement. It is hoped that this teacher praise and experience of achievement, which are natural to a classroom setting, will act as reinforcement to maintain this volunteering to do board work—even when the edibles have been faded to omission.

In preparing to move toward the use of "natural" reinforcement, it is useful to pair words of encouragement and praise with the delivery of tangible reinforcement. For example, while "rewarding" a student by allowing her to engage in preferred activities after completion of assigned work, it is helpful to accompany this with a statement such as, "You really did an excellent job today. You should be really proud of yourself." Again, it is this type of verbal praise that will naturally occur within the classroom and will help maintain the target behavior.

The following case illustration of a student, self-described as having problems talking with girls, demonstrates the process of developing a target behavior through shaping and systematic use of contingent reinforcement (Case Illustration 3.1).

Case Illustration 3.1   Mark: Difficulty Talking to Girls

Consider the case of a tenth-grade student, Mark, who came to the counselor because of his self-described problem of "talking to girls." Baseline data revealed that Mark was able to engage with his classmates, both male and female, in situations regarding academic task achievement. While able to interact with his male friends in social situations, Mark became quiet, withdrawn, and avoidant when in the presence of female classmates.

Setting Goals

While the reduction of this social anxiety and the development of social skills was a desirable goal, the student wanted to initially work on the specific goal of asking Lauren, a girl in his class, to go to the homecoming dance. Apparently, Mark has received feedback from his friends that Lauren would like to go to the dance with Mark, but Mark has never asked a girl out and is finding the possibility of asking Lauren to the dance to be somewhat daunting. With this set as the terminal goal, a system of shaping was developed, using the following subgoals.

1. To be physically present when his friends hang out with Lauren and her friends during lunch.

2. To look at Lauren when she speaks.

3. To ask Lauren a question and/or expand on her disclosure.

4. To approach Lauren with a question about a class project.

(Continued)

(Continued)

5. To talk to Lauren about a nonacademic issue—for example, discuss the upcoming band competition (since they are both in the marching band), or her feelings about the football game, etc.

6. To ask Lauren about the homecoming preparations, since she is on the homecoming committee.

7. To ask Lauren if she is intending to go to the homecoming dance.

8. To ask Lauren if she would like to go to the dance with him.

Identifying and Employing Reinforcement

With these as target behaviors, the counselor and student discussed ways that Mark could be rewarded for performing the desired behavior. Initially, Mark felt that he didn't need any "payoffs," but as each goal was reviewed, it became evident that even these tasks were difficult for him to perform and, as such, some immediate payoff may prove useful. Mark felt confident that if he could ask Lauren to the dance, Lauren would say yes, and as a result he decided to take the flyer announcing the homecoming dance and cut it into eight small pieces, making it into a jigsaw puzzle. In a very creative approach to reinforcement, Mark decided that each time he successfully achieved a subgoal, he would randomly select one of the eight pieces of the flyer and begin to assemble as if it were a puzzle. He felt that the developing picture of the homecoming announcement would serve as reinforcement for his continued movement toward the terminal goal of asking Lauren to the dance.

Over the course of a two-week period, Mark and his counselor would meet to discuss his progress and the value of the puzzle-piece reward system. Mark gave evidence of his excitement about the puzzle-piece reward system, noting that he created a place on his desk that he was using to allow the flyer to take form.

During one session, the counselor was able to highlight the "natural" reinforcements Mark had experienced and could experience as a result of engaging in social encounters. For example, Mark noted that in one incident Lauren was talking about a cd she purchased, and in an attempt to accomplish his third subgoal, he expanded on her discussion by stating that he had actually seen the band (American HiFi) in concert. That disclosure encouraged Lauren and Megan (Lauren's friend) to begin to actively ask Mark about the band and the concert. Their interest in his music taste and experience was extremely pleasurable and served as a major reinforcement to his social engagement. This point was reflected and highlighted by the counselor as natural payoff for engaging in social encounters.

In addition to "earning" his third puzzle piece, this experience allowed Mark to actually skip two of the previously identified subgoals (4 and 5) and move directly to engaging with Lauren about the homecoming preparations, with specific discussion focusing on the type of music that would be played. The experience of shared music interest and the pleasant exchanges experienced made the transition to step 8, asking Lauren to the dance, smooth and easy to achieve.

Following-Up

In follow-up with the Mark, the counselor provided encouragement and support for his efforts, and again highlighted the natural payoffs he was experiencing by engaging in this form of social exchange. Not only did Mark have a date for the dance, but now other girls, including Megan, began to speak with him in class and at lunch.

The counselor reviewed the process employed and helped Mark understand the value of taking terminal goals and breaking them in smaller, achievable approximations (i.e., shaping), which, if followed by reinforcement, would facilitate achievement of any terminal goal.

TOKEN ECONOMY: INCREASING IMMEDIACY AND AVOIDING SATIATION

Clearly, the use of reinforcement as a strategy for fostering the development and maintenance of a desired behavior is not a simple process. Questions and concerns such as what would constitute reinforcement for this or that student; or how can it be delivered immediately; and how do we insure need satisfaction, yet avoid satiation, serve as focal points for counselor's reflective practice. One approach often employed to address these issues of immediacy and satiation is the use of a *token economy*.

Token systems or token economies operate with two core elements. The first element is the employment of a token that is a tangible symbol and can be delivered easily and immediately following the demonstration of the target behavior(s). The second core element to a token economy is the presence of a "menu" of desirable activities, privileges, and items—and by its very breadth and variety, the menu reduces the chances of satiation.

Consider a very common form of "token system" for which we are all very much aware . . . our own monetary system. The dollar bill that one receives as a result of performing a desired behavior has no real need-satisfying value, in and of itself. However, people will perform work in order to receive these dollar bills—because they serve as the medium of exchange for other events, items, and experiences that can be acquired at a later date and do meet the individual's needs. In this case, the dollar is a token—an item that can be collected and exchanged for meaningful objects or privileges. While counselors will not be distributing "dollars" to students, a token system will look like any "economy" in that there will be a medium of exchange, a schedule or rate of exchange and goods and services which can be "purchased." In developing a token system, whether it is used for an individual or a group (e.g., an entire class), a number of elements must be included.

Targeting Behavior

For the system to be effective, the student needs to know exactly which behaviors result in the reception of tokens (reinforcement). As such, prior to implementing a token economy, the counselor and student need to discuss and agree upon the system to be employed. As with all behavioral interventions, token systems are most effective when the target behavior is defined in specific terms (e.g., "raising hand in class") rather than general terms (e.g., "being good"), and when the behavior is measurable (e.g., minutes engaged in proper behavior, percentage correct, etc.).

Identifying Tokens

A token can be anything that is visible and countable. While it is of value to make the token attractive, it is most important that the token is easy to dispense and difficult to counterfeit. Some counselors have used special poker chips, or bingo chips, or even have creatively manufactured "play money." Other commonly used items include stickers, point tallies, check marks, or buttons.

Identifying Back-Up Reinforcers

Back-up reinforcers are the meaningful objects, privileges, or activities that the student can receive in exchange for tokens. In developing a menu of back-up reinforcers, the counselor should enlist the student for suggestions of items and privileges, which are attractive to that student. It is also useful to identify items and privileges that are "natural" to the school environment. For example, while a third-grade student may like to be taken for ice cream, the same student may find being first in line for lunch, or being assigned the task serving as attendance reporter, equally desirable. The use of the "natural" items and privileges insures their availability for future maintenance of the desired behavior.

Establishing an Exchange Rate and System

A system including specification of time, place, and rate of exchange needs to be established. The token value of each back-up reinforcer is predetermined based on monetary value, demand, or therapeutic value. For example, if the reinforcer is expensive or highly attractive, the token value should be higher. If possession of, or participation in, the reinforcing item or activity would aid in the individual's acquisition of targeted or other desirable skills, the token value should be lower. For example, the student who is working on increasing her social skills will find that a "ticket" to the dance has a lower exchange rate than the opportunity to engage in some socially isolating behavior (e.g., playing a video game). It is important that the student has the opportunity to both earn tokens and to exchange even a minimal amount of tokens for some form of back-up reinforcer. Thus, the menu should include exchange items that can be acquired with very few tokens, as well as other items that have a higher token-value.

Implementing a Token System

Once the system is in place, the counselor and student will agree upon the way of recording data reflecting the performance of the desired behavior and the plan for awarding of the tokens. Initially, as the new behavior is just starting to be developed, tokens are awarded frequently and in higher amounts. As the performance of the desired behavior becomes more natural, more routine within the student's behavioral repertoire, the opportunities to earn tokens decrease. By gradually decreasing the availability of tokens, the student will learn to display the desirable behaviors independently, simply for the satisfaction experienced in performing those behaviors and/or for the natural self or other praise received as a result of performing those behaviors.

Case Illustration 3.2 demonstrates the use of a token economy system with a group of high school students who had a problem with school attendance. The illustration is brief, and those interested in a more detailed explication of the use of token economies with individuals and entire groups should review the work of Jenson, Sloan, and Young (1988); and Sulzer-Azaroff and Mayer (1996).

| Case Illustration 3.2 | Robert: A Counselor Reducing School Absenteeism and Tardiness |

In addition to an already burgeoning caseload and set of work assignments, Robert, the seniors' counselor, was asked to work with thirty-two seniors who had been identified by the dean of students and the principal as potential dropouts. Needless to say, thirty-two special referrals added to an overloaded case listing was a difficult task to manage. Robert enlisted the assistance of the department secretary to serve, along with Robert, in implementing a token economy targeting the increase of student punctuality and attendance.

Intervention Design

As an initial step to the development of a token economy system to employ with these thirty-two students, the department secretary surveyed several classes of seniors asking them to rank in order of preference a list of possible rewards (see Figure 3.1).

(Continued)

(Continued)

The students were also invited to write down other desirable items or activities which they felt would be attractive as rewards. This listing provided the raw material from which backup reinforcers were established.

Backup reinforcers were grouped into one of two categories: (1) privileges, such as getting early dismissal or free time during study hall; and (2) tangibles, such as lunch tokens, or supplies from the student store.

Figure 3.1 Sample Survey for Back-Up Reinforcers

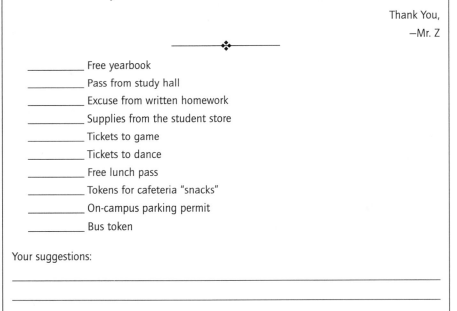

Survey of "Valued" Items and Privileges

Below are listed a number of items, or activities, most of which can be found here at school. Please rank each item in order of preference to you. Place #1 next to the item you value the most, #2 next to the one you feel would be next in value, and so on. At the end of the list, we have left spaces for your suggestions of things (activities, objects, or privileges) that you feel would be of value to you but are not listed.

Thank You,

—Mr. Z

❖

_____ Free yearbook

_____ Pass from study hall

_____ Excuse from written homework

_____ Supplies from the student store

_____ Tickets to game

_____ Tickets to dance

_____ Free lunch pass

_____ Tokens for cafeteria "snacks"

_____ On-campus parking permit

_____ Bus token

Your suggestions:

_____

_____

_____

Implementation

During the initial session, students were informed about the program, the program goals, and the reinforcement contingencies. The students were told that the record of their class attendance and punctuality would be sent to the department secretary every afternoon. Furthermore, they were told that they would receive two points for each class they attended on time, and one point for any class they attended, but arrived late (an absence would mean that no points would be rewarded for that class). This system allowed each student to earn a maximum of 14 points (i.e., 7 classes) each day. The students were told that at the end of the school day, points accrued for that day would be recorded using a check-mark system and that the totals would be posted on a special bulletin board.

The exchange rate and backup-reinforcement menu was next explained. Students were told that each check mark would be "worth" 25-cent credit toward an item in the student store or lunchroom. In addition, students were told that privileges could also be earned as part of the token system and copies of the specific menu and exchange rates (see Figure 3.2) were distributed. This menu and exchange rate was also posted in the exchange room (at the secretary's desk).

Figure 3.2 • Sample Token-Exchange Menu

Exchange Rate and Menu

The items listed below can be purchased though exchange of the tokens you have earned. The specific exchange rate is listed for many items, however, for the items which have a variable dollar figure, the number of tokens required will be based on an exchange rate of one token = $0.25 value. For example, if you wish to get a school t-shirt, which costs $15.00 at the student store, you will be required to exchange 60 tokens.

Item	Exchange Rate
Supplies from student store	Exchange rate: 1 token = 25 cent equivalent
Lunch pass	8 tokens
Free snack chips (tokens)	2 tokens per each snack chip
Pass from study hall	4 tokens per period
Pass to media center/library during study hall	2 tokens per period
Exemption from cafeteria clean-up duty	6 tokens
Excuse from written homework (with teacher permission)	8 tokens
Sports event ticket	8 tokens
Dance ticket	6 tokens
Bus pass	6 tokens
School yearbook	160 tokens

(Continued)

(Continued)

Finally, the students were informed about the mechanics of the exchange. The students were allowed to come to the secretary's desk any day between 2:40 and 3:30 in order to exchange their token (check marks) for back-up reinforcers. The students would sign their name, and the time they arrived, in a book on the secretary's desk. When she called their name they could make the exchange(s), sign the time in the book, and then leave.

Results

Of the students invited to participate, nine students initially protested that the program was childish, and elected not to participate. These students were scheduled to meet one-on-one with a counselor to discuss their absenteeism and they were informed that they would be allowed to participate if they changed their mind at a later date. Throughout the twelve weeks of the program, seven of the initial reluctant joined the program.

All of the students participating in the program (n = 30) improved on their punctuality and attendance. An interesting and unexpected finding was that following the first week of exchanges, the students decided that a more pleasant outcome would be to simply see who could earn the most points. It appeared that the competition was more of a payoff than the original listing of backup reinforcers.

SUMMARY

Understanding the Behavioral Deficit

- Quite often, the student presenting at the counselor's office does so with deficit or deficiency in terms of his or her behavioral options.
- The intervention of choice would be the systematic employment of reinforcement to develop and maintain the desired behaviors.

Programming for Growth

The degree to which the employment of operant techniques is successful is to a large extent a function of the counselor's ability to use data to guide his or her systematic application of the following behavioral principles:

- Selecting a target behavior: specifying the desired behavior in concrete, measurable terms that assure that the reinforcement program can be applied consistently and that real change can be noted.

- Using shaping: also known as the method of successive approximations, defining the gradual modification of a behavior reinforcing successive approximations of the desired behavior.
- Selecting reinforcers: not as simple nor as easy as one may think, as it is intuitively appealing to state that things such as candy, stickers, good grades, and special attention are "rewards" for students, yet the truth is we only know a reward—a reinforcement—by the way it acts. This is a very important concept. A reinforcement is only a reinforcement *if* it strengthens the behavior that led to its reception.

Implementing Immediacy and Contingency

- Since by definition, reinforcement is that which increases the frequency or intensity of the behavior that led to it, it is essential to close the time gap between the performance of the behavior and the reception of the reinforcement.

Employing Natural Reinforcement

- As the target behavior increases, the counselor plans for transitioning from the "artificial" reinforcement that has been employed to identifying contingencies in the natural environment, and then makes sure the terminal behavior is trapped (i.e., maintained) by these consequences.

Creating a Token Economy

- One approach often employed to address these issues of immediacy and satiation is the use of a token economy.
- Token systems or token economies operate with two core elements. The first element is the employment of a token as a tangible symbol that can be delivered easily and immediately following the demonstration of the target behavior(s). The second core element to a token economy is the presence of a "menu" of desirable activities, privileges, and items—which by its very breadth and variety reduces the chances of satiation.

Strategies Targeting **4** the Reduction and/or Elimination of Behavior

S tudents, or those sharing concern for them, may seek assistance with the reduction, if not outright elimination, of undesired and maladaptive behaviors. Even when the behavior of concern is one that the student him- or herself seeks to reduce or eliminate, it must be remembered that even these troublesome and problematic behaviors serve some function or purpose for the student. As with the acquisition and maintenance of desirable behaviors, undesirable behaviors are most likely acquired and maintained as a result of being reinforced.

Often, students' inappropriate behaviors are inadvertently rewarded or reinforced. This would be the case when the student's acting out in the classroom results in her receiving the teacher's attention that she desired, or when the pain of social anxiety is removed whenever the student engages in drinking. While the behaviors are clearly not those desired, they are in fact functional in providing need satisfaction for the student.

In general, strategies that either weaken the reinforcer following the undesirable behavior or strengthen the reinforcement for an alternative, more desirable behavior (Miltenberger, 1997) are useful interventions for reducing undesirable behaviors. This chapter discusses four such strategies: extinction, differential reinforcement, flooding, and punishment.

EXTINCTION

Mrs. Raphael, Lydia's second-grade teacher, comes to the counselor's office to share her concern about Lydia's "immaturity." In dialogue with

63

the counselor, the teacher describes a situation in which Lydia often stamps her foot loudly on the classroom floor, whenever she doesn't get the teacher's attention. Mrs. Raphael explains that she has spoken to Lydia about this behavior and yet it seems to be getting worse. Under these conditions, the teacher's attention is exactly the payoff Lydia's seeks.

Often, adults fail to recognize that they encourage these behaviors by giving students attention when they do them. The attention can be as simple as eye contact, sighing, or scolding the student. It would appear that Lydia's behavior may in fact begin to diminish if and when it no longer works to gain the teacher's attention. This is the basis for a process of extinction.

Extinction is the first step in the behavior analysis continuum of procedures that strives to decrease misbehaviors. Extinction of operant behavior involves the termination of the reinforcement contingency that maintains the response. Extinction is the least intrusive procedure in this continuum, and as a result, can take some time for the behavior to stop. The overall outcome of extinction is a reduction or elimination of the operant response (O'Reilly, Lancioni, & Taylor, 1999). For Lydia, the operant behavior (i.e., stamping her foot) that had been maintained by the resulting teacher attention will be reduced once that reinforcement is no longer "delivered" following the exhibition of the operant stamping.

It may appear counterintuitive to an unknowing teacher, parent, or counselor, who assumes that his or her "negative" attention will naturally reduce the behavior, to embrace the fact that his or her "negative" attention is actually maintaining the problem behavior. It simply doesn't make sense to suggest that "reprimands" or "nasty looks" or pleas to cease and desist are actually positively reinforcing the inappropriate behavior. But, the proof is in the outcome. If the behaviors that resulted in the experience of these conditions (i.e., reprimands, nasty look, etc.) increases in frequency, we know that, by definition, they have been reinforced!

Extinction procedures work well with students who whine, complain, cling, throw tantrums, or call out. But extinction procedures can sometimes prove effective with students exhibiting inappropriate social behaviors, for example, seduction. Consider the experience of the high school counselor working with Sherry, a ninth-grade student who would often make inappropriate flirtatious remarks while sitting with the counselor. Previous efforts to ask her to cease seemed only to increase her engagement in this process. The counselor decided to break eye contact, make no facial expression, and redirect the conversation when presented with these comments. As Sherry increased appropriate disclosures, the counselor returned to engaging with the student, even remarking how much he enjoyed working with her. This process of increasing attention and engagement when Sherry was appropriate as well as ignoring and disengaging when she would make flirtatious responses successfully eliminated the presence of these undesirable responses in session.

Two Approaches to Extinction

The fundamental process of extinction entails removing and/or breaking the association of a reinforcement with the undesirable behavior. Thus, extinction can be accomplished in one of two ways. First, and most traditionally, extinction can occur by *omission.* That is, when reinforcement is completely removed or omitted the target behavior will be reduced.

Extinction by omission requires that all reinforcement in response to the student's misbehavior is removed. This may seem like a relatively innocuous statement, but one must remember that some behaviors are self-reinforcing and thus not available for reinforcement removal. Or perhaps, others within the setting, for example, peers, provide reinforcement beyond that offered the teacher. In this latter situation, the counselor would have to insure that the student's peers also removed their attention and encouragement following the performance of the misbehavior if it is to be successfully extinguished.

A second approach to extinction is to break the contingent association between the behavior and the reinforcer (O'Reilly et al., 1999). In this approach, the consequent stimulus that historically reinforced the problem behavior is delivered on a response-independent or time-based schedule. This form of extinction has been referred to as noncontingent reinforcement (NCR) (Vollmer, Iwata, Zarcone, Smith, & Mazaleski, 1993).

The assumption underlying noncontingent reinforcement as an intervention for reducing a behavior is that since the inappropriate behavior has proven effective in acquiring some desirable consequence, experiencing that consequence irrespective of the behavior will break the link between the inappropriate behavior and the desired consequence. If, for example, the desirable consequence of receiving teacher attention is given irrespective of the student's behavior, the link or contingency that had been created would not longer be salient.

In studies comparing extinction by omission and noncontingent reinforcement, misbehaviors treated with NCR resulted in a faster decrease of the unwanted behavior and fewer recurrences (Vollmer et al., 1993; O'Reilly et al., 1999). Case Illustration 4.1 provides a brief illustration of this process.

Case Illustration 4.1   Alicia: Noncontingent Reinforcement

Alicia was a fifteen-year-old, tenth-grade student who exhibited intermittent explosive behavior. In session, any time the counselor would attempt to set a direction or pursue a topic of interest, Alicia would slam her fist on a desk and utter an obscenity. The counselor's initial reaction to this behavior was to invite Alicia to talk about her feelings, an invitation which was most often met by Alicia setting a direction and topic for the session and the counselor merely following. It appeared that Alicia's outbursts were reinforced by the counselor's attending to Alicia's agenda.

In discussing this with her supervisor (the department chair), the school counselor decided to implement a process of ignoring Alicia's outbursts while applying noncontingent reinforcement, in the form of providing Alicia invitations to set the tone and direction for discussion, at random times throughout the session.

Counselor: (Ignores the outburst.) So, if I understand what your teacher, Ms. Rutts, is saying, she is concerned that you sometimes have trouble participating with your group.

Alicia: (Hits the table.)

Counselor: (Ignores the behavior.) I was hoping you could help me understand what is happening in group.

Alicia   (States an obscenity in reference to the group.)

Counselor: (Ignores the outburst.) I was guessing that maybe you were having a problem understanding what the group is doing? Or, then I thought maybe some of the members of the groups were not including you in the discussion? But these are just my guesses.

Alicia: (Screaming) I don't want to talk about it!

Counselor: I understand that you don't want to talk about it. I sure wish you did because then you and I could figure out how to make the work in your group a lot more enjoyable.

Alicia: Yeah, right! How?

The counselor, having ignored the outbursts, has invited Alicia to engage in a discussion of the behavior of concern. This discussion continues for a few minutes, with Alicia answering the counselor's questions regarding the nature of the group work.

Counselor: Well, you know what? We can talk more about this later, and I bet we can figure things out to make it a lot more enjoyable for you—but I'd love to find out more about you (giving Alicia control over the discussion direction). I mean, like what are some of your favorite things to do?

This noncontingent experience of "control," when paired with the counselor's ignoring of Alicia's outbursts, successfully reduced this explosive behavior in session.

Buyer Beware!

While the research clearly supports the effectiveness of extinction procedures in reducing undesirable behaviors, there are a couple of caveats to the employment of this strategy that the counselor needs to understand.

First, extinction procedures should never be used if the student is in real physical distress, in harm's way, may be a danger to others, or when the environmental situation just isn't conducive to this technique. Secondly, it is essential for the counselor to understand the possible responses a student may exhibit when extinction is employed. The most predictable response is that the behavior gets worse before it improves. This is an important consideration when deciding on the use of extinction as a strategy for reducing undesirable behavior.

It is not unusual for a student to increase the frequency and/or intensity of the undesired behavior (O'Reilly et al., 1999) when extinction is employed. This increase has been termed an "extinction burst," and represents a student's last ditch effort to regain the reinforcement previously experienced.

It is not atypical for a student to engage in more exaggerated forms of the misbehavior (Shukla-Mehta & Albin, 2003). Thus, the student who received teacher attention following the making of "burping sounds" may begin actually to call out, employ obscenities, or bang items as an escalated form of her previous attention-getting behavior once extinction procedures are instituted.

The possibility of this "extinction burst" needs to be understood and considered in the decision-making process. The danger is that if unprepared and/or unable to continue to withhold the reinforcement (continuing extinction) during this "burst," then what happens is that not only has the behavior not been reduced, but in fact more exaggerated forms have been reinforced and strengthened. It is essential *not* to engage in extinctions unless time, conditions, and ability support the adherence to this process.

DIFFERENTIAL REINFORCEMENT

Extinction is, or can be, an effective strategy for reducing undesirable behaviors. But it is important to remember that these behaviors, while being identified as undesirable, remain functional. Even these identified behaviors of concern worked at some level to provide the student something he or she wanted. Thus, if we attempt to eliminate a behavior without attending to the purpose it served, we may find that the behavior reappears or another behavior, perhaps one even less desirable, may take its place in order to achieve the same end. When planning on removing these behaviors, it is helpful to simultaneously plan on developing an alternative, more desirable behavior that will serve a similar function. This was the approach employed by the counselor working with Bailey (Case Illustration 4.2).

Case Illustration 4.2   Bailey: Differential Reinforcement

Bailey was a first-grade student who exhibited disruptive behavior when confronted with a period of transition from one school activity to another. Bailey would exhibit verbal tantrums, making loud proclamations that "I won't do it" or "I don't want to" or simply "No!" Her responses were at a volume and pitch that proved disruptive to the other children.

The counselor's observation and functional analysis suggested that Bailey's preferred activities involved the use of manipulatives and/or art supplies. Whereas any time the class was directed to reading circle, an area of pillows arranged in the corner of the room, Bailey would express her resistance and displeasure by engaging in verbal tantrums.

Bailey showed a preference for working with clay and crayons, so these items were chosen as reinforcements for compliance to teacher direction for transition to the reading circle. The counselor worked with the teacher and an intervention plan was established which entailed ignoring Bailey's tantrums while directing the other students to the reading area. However, as soon as Bailey stopped the verbal refusal and began movement to the circle, she was handed a crayon or stick of clay that she could include in her art box for that day's art activity. The distribution of the crayon was accompanied by the teacher's verbal reinforcement, for example: "Bailey, I am happy you are joining us."

On the initial employment of this extinction and differential reinforcement program, Bailey began to increase her vocal volume to a point where she was actually screaming in protest (extinction bump). However, the teacher, teacher's aide, and other students continued to move to the reading circle without attending to Bailey. Bailey sat quietly, watching the students take up their pillows. As soon as the children sat in circle, Bailey came and took the pillow next to the teacher, an action for which she received a crayon and the teacher's praise. ("Bailey, thank you for quietly joining us.") Within three days of implementing this process, Bailey's verbal tantrums when invited to transition to reading time were eliminated.

Differential reinforcement procedures involve reinforcing an alternative behavior, often incompatible to the targeted BORC, while simultaneously extinguishing the targeted problematic behavior. Kazdin (2001) noted that rewarding "incompatible" behaviors could lead to more rapid change in challenging behaviors. Research on the use of differential-reinforcement procedures (e.g., Purdie, Hattie, & Carroll, 2002) has consistently demonstrated their effectiveness as strategies for the reduction of undesirable behavior.

FLOODING

Flooding is an intervention technique demonstrated to be an effective and economical method for rapidly reducing undesirable behavior (Spiegler & Guevremont, 1998). The key to this procedure is the rapid, condensed exposure to the troublesome stimuli or situation.

While the technique is most often employed within a clinical setting, as will be noted, it can be an effective strategy employed by a *trained* school counselor within the school setting. For example, a counselor working with a student with an intense fear and aversion of elevators, and who now, because of being on crutches, is required to use the school elevator, may get her on the elevator, first with the counselor and then alone. Repeated elevator trips, perhaps a half a dozen to a dozen within a condensed time period of thirty minutes, would "flood" the student with the fear signal but in the process desensitize her to its previously fear-inducing quality. This concentrated experience of the previously associated fear situation *in the absence* of real pain or harmful outcome results in a reduction of the fear response.

Another situation in which flooding may be an appropriate strategy for the school counselor to use is that of school refusal. The use of rapid return to school (a form of flooding) has been suggested, especially in situations where school refusal has had an acute onset. Research (e.g., King, Heyne, Tonge, Gullone, & Ollendick, 2001) has demonstrated the effectiveness of such rapid return when employed with school refusal cases of varying severity. For example, Rebecca, a first-grade student, refuses to go to school, following her first-week experience. It appears that Rebecca was teased by the older (third-grade) students during the first week of school and now "pleads" with her mother not to go back. In working with Rebecca's mother, the counselor suggests that the she bring Rebecca back to school. The counselor explains that it is important to be empathetic to her daughter's distress and affirm that things will be okay, but that under no conditions of her pleading should she give in to Rebecca's request to stay home. Subsequently, when Rebecca arrives at school, the counselor meets her at the door and takes Rebecca to her office. During this initial encounter, Rebecca continues to protest and plead to go home. The counselor shares her understanding of Rebecca's upset, while at the same time ignoring the pleas to go home. As Rebecca begins to calm, the counselor directs her to a table in the office, where there is "deskwork" that her teacher prepared and sent to the counselor's office.

At the appropriate time, the counselor takes Rebecca to her "lunch" period and requests that the teacher direct Rebecca to her classroom following lunch, where she stays until the end of the day. This procedure is followed in subsequent days, with one exception. The time spent with the counselor in her office is shortened and eventually eliminated, as is the process of meeting Rebecca at the door. Now that Rebecca is back in school, the counselor follows up to discuss the teasing and alternative ways that Rebecca can use to respond to such situations.

The fact that this strategy, by definition, exposes the student to the fear stimuli that he or she has been avoiding makes informed consent a must. The student needs to understand that while no harm will come to him or her, he or she will most likely encounter discomfort. *It must be highlighted that only school counselors who have been specifically trained and supervised in the use of this technique should consider its use in practice.*

EXPOSURE AND RESPONSE PREVENTION

Exposure and response prevention, or ERP, is a behavioral strategy often used when intervening with students experiencing debilitating anxiety. ERP is predicated on the belief that anxiety can be reduced or extinguished if the student is confronted by his or her fear stimuli, and prevented from escaping the situation under a condition where there is no accompanying pain or danger. The model proposes that a student's avoidance or escape behaviors, while appearing to provide short-term relief, are in fact supporting the maintenance of the fear response. Consider, for example, a student who responds to the sight of a dog by running away, terrified. Once gaining distance between the dog and himself, the student will most likely experience a reduction in anxiety. This reduction in anxiety serves as a reinforcement for the running-away behavior, and thus strengthens that behavior in response to sight of a dog. However, if that student were able to stay in the presence of this friendly dog, he would also experience the fact that the fear stimulus (i.e., the dog) is *not* associated with danger or painful attack. It is this experience, this pairing of the previously feared signal with the absence of pain will result in the extinction of the anxiety response to the sight of a dog—an extinction that is prevented by the student's own escape/avoidance responses.

Students often come to counseling because their avoidance behaviors or use of ritualistic behaviors (e.g., hand washing, recurrent checking, etc.), while serving to alleviate anxiety, have now become problematic in themselves. For example, consider Jim, a student who is failing many of his classes because of what appears to be his unwillingness or inability to complete his deskwork assignments. When baseline data are collected, it becomes clear that Jim's difficulty with completing deskwork is due to his excessive checking behavior. It appears that each time he is presented with an assignment, Jim becomes flooded with anxiety about doing the task incorrectly. His way of dealing with this anxiety is to perform multiple checking of all his work. While initially such checking served a useful purpose in that it did allow him to correct his work prior to handing it in, it now occurs with such frequency that it is creating a host of problems for Jim, including an inability to complete the assigned tasks. Jim continues to do the checking and rechecking as a ritual geared to protecting him from failing. The problem is that he is now trapped in his response to the initial anxieties about failure, and this now actually prevents him from ever testing whether "failure" would actually occur, if he didn't check.

As another illustration, consider the student who has learned to anticipate social encounters to be painfully humiliating. This student may develop strategies geared to help her avoid social encounters—whether the encounter would or would not, in fact, be painful and humiliating. The very action of avoiding and/or escaping social situations prevents this student from ever coming to realize that any one particular social encounter would or would not have been painful. The very process of avoiding allows the student to maintain her anticipation of painful humiliation and never have it challenged by actual experience.

Under these conditions, the logical intervention would thus involve an element of engaging the student with the feared situation. The persistent exposure to the feared item, when done in a condition of *absence* of accompanying pain or danger, will result in a reduction of the anxiety. The "exposure" part of this treatment involves either direct or imagined controlled exposure to objects or situations that trigger the anxiety. Over time, exposure to these objects or situations leads to less and less anxiety. But for this reduction to occur, the student cannot escape or avoid the exposure. Thus, the second part of the process is the "response prevention." The "response" in "response prevention" refers to the repetitive and often ritualized behaviors employed by the student to escape and or avoid the anxiety. This process is illustrated in Case Illustration, 4.3.

Case Illustration 4.3   Michelle: ERP With OCD

Michelle, a fourteen-year-old, ninth-grade student, came to the counselor explaining that she was unable to concentrate and remain in class because every time she touched her desk top, a place that others students had used in previous classes, she became intensely afraid of catching something and needed to leave to wash her hands. Clearly, the constant request to leave the room not only took her out of the learning situation, raised concerns and reactions from her peers, but the experienced anxiety also was a block to her learning and achievement.

(Continued)

(Continued)

The counselor and the student agreed to the use of ERP as an intervention for this anxiety and ritualistic hand washing. In the initial session, the student received information about the procedure and the fact that initially the steps taken may elevate anxiety, but that with perseverance the anxiety would peak and then diminish. Michelle gave consent and the process was initiated in the second session.

Counselor:	Well, Michelle let's begin, using our scale—how are you feeling right now?
Michelle:	A bit nervous. I think maybe a 7 or 8. But I want to do this. I really do.
Counselor:	It's not unusual to be a bit nervous, but as we discussed last time, if you can "sit" with the anxiety, it will dissipate, and there will be nothing that we do that will place you in any real danger. So if you are ready, I would like you to get as comfortable as you can in the chair (reaching into a bag and produces a school textbook). That's great. Michelle, I want you to place your hand on this book. This book belongs to another student.
Michelle:	Do I have to hold it or can I just touch it with the tip of my finger?
Counselor:	(Hands the student the book.) No, as we discussed before, I want you to hold the book and actually, I would like you to rub your hands all over the book. See if you can have the cover touch every part of your hand.
Michelle:	I'm getting that weird feeling. I don't think I want to do this . . .
Counselor:	(Reflects "in" session, and concludes that Michelle needs to be reminded of the process and the importance of not quitting in process; and also to see Michelle's "talking" as a possible escape process.) Michelle, I can understand this is making you uncomfortable, but as we discussed last time, you will feel an increase in anxiety but it will reduce if you stay with it. Stopping now would not be good. So, I would like you to not talk, but rather look at the book, see its colors, the design on the cover. I want you to focus on how it feels as you place your fingers—your palm—on the cover. Identify its texture. Just quietly focus on the experience for a few moments.
Counselor:	(Remains quiet.)
Michelle:	This is hard.
Counselor:	You are doing really well—focus now—try to concentrate on the actual sensations you have touching the book. Yes, that's it. Try to rub the cover over the back of your hands . . . in between your fingers . . . excellent (remaining quiet, while student focuses on the sensation). Super, Michelle. Where would you place yourself on our scale?
Michelle:	I'm at about a 7 or 8 . . . this is hard.
Counselor:	I know, but you are doing well. That's it . . . rub hands on the book . . . get the cover to touch in between your fingers . . .

In the case of Michelle, the counselor needed to be alert to the student's subtle attempts to escape the anxiety-provoking situation. While it may be expected that the student would express the desire to stop the process, as a way of escaping the situation, her attempt to engage the counselor in dialogue may have also been an escape strategy. That is, as they talked about the process, she was not focusing on the actual experience—that of touching the book—and thus reduced the anxiety at the moment. The counselor needs to be sure the student understands the importance of staying with the process, before actually engaging in it. Further, it is important to be alert to the student's need for support and encouragement in session and at the same time, know when to refocus the student back to the anxiety and the anxiety-provoking event. As the sessions continues, the counselor will move from having Michelle touch something only very mildly "contaminated," to gradually increasing the intensity of the stimuli during the exposure phase.

Throughout the process, the counselor supports and encourages the student, focusing on the discomfort being experienced while encouraging the student to resist performance of the ritualistic behavior, allowing the anxiety to dissipate on its own. The student habituates, that is, gets used to the (formerly) anxiety-producing situation, and discovers that her anxiety level has dropped considerably. As this occurs, they can then progress to touching something more "contaminated" without performing the ritual behavior of washing.

The counselor employing such a program needs a very specific behavioral plan, which includes elaborate and extensive student education to the rationale and value of this procedure. It is important for the counselor to be sensitive to the fact that the process is one aimed at intentionally not allowing the student to use his or her coping mechanism. Even though this coping behavior, for example, ritualistic washing, has been identified as a behavior of real concern and maladaptive, it remains the student's method of coping. Thus the student, while understanding the need to refrain from avoidance or rituals, must also be helped to tolerate the discomfort that will initially be experienced. The student will need to know that gradually and with repeated exposures, the experience will climb, peak, and subside. *Further, it must be highlighted that only school counselors who have been specifically trained and supervised in the use of this technique should consider its use in practice.*

What follows are the steps to be taken by a counselor reflecting "on" ERP practice, but as with any such technique, the use of ERP by a school counselor is contingent on having the appropriate training and supervision as well as school sanctioning.

Step 1. Explaining the Process and Value of ERP and Establishing the Schedule

During the initial session, the student will receive help understanding how the tendency to avoid anxiety-provoking situations and/or employ rituals as a way of "escaping" are behaviors which are (a) ineffective at reducing anxiety in the long-term, (b) interfering with normal functioning, and (c) preventing him or her from developing more effective strategies for coping with anxiety. The counselor will explain to the student the specific details of how the counseling will proceed, and the student is encouraged to ask questions and share all concerns. During this introduction and explanation, the utility of the hierarchy is explained in the context of the exposure-response prevention model, which involves gradually exposing the student to anxiety-provoking situations while he or she refrains from engagement in escape or avoidance behaviors. The student is informed that such a process results in habituation to anxiety, as his or her anxiety attenuates without reliance on compensatory ritualistic behavior. The student is told that the sessions will start with a minimally to moderately distressing situation and progress up the hierarchy during subsequent exposures. Sometimes it helps to provide the student with a visual aid or an analogy such as climbing a ladder, as a way of illustrating the hierarchical presentation.

One rather unique characteristic of this approach is that sessions are often scheduled for ninety minutes in length and scheduled in subsequent days rather than weeks. Research (e.g., Franklin, Tolin, March, & Foa, 2001) suggests that prolonged, continuous exposures are superior to shorter, intermittent exposures. Such a scheduling format may prove prohibitive, given the typical caseloads and schedules employed by most school counselors.

Step 2. Developing an Exposure Hierarchy

When reflecting "on" practice, the behavioral counselor intending to implement ERP strategy will work with the student to create a list of the stimuli that elicit the anxiety response. These situations are ranked on a scale of 0 (representing the situation producing the least anxiety) to 10 (representing the situation of highest anxiety). In addition, students are usually asked to rate their level of anxiety in each situation on a scale from 0 (no anxiety or discomfort) to 100 (extreme anxiety and discomfort). This scale is called the subjective units of distress scale, or SUDS. As illustrated in the case of Michelle, students may be asked to provide SUDS ratings at regular intervals during exposure treatment, for example every five minutes.

Using Michelle as our sample case, her initial hierarchy may look like the following:

1. Touching her own book as it rests on the desk.

2. Touching a piece of paper resting on the desk.

3. Touching her own book that has been in on the desk.

4. Touching another's book that has been on the desk.

5. Touching the desk with the tip of her finger, etc.

Step 3. Presenting the Response Prevention

During the initial exposure session, the counselor will attempt to start with a situation with a low SUDS rating in order to provide the student with maximal opportunity for success. It is important to remind the student that, during the exposure, he or she may experience some anxiety but highlight how important it is from the student to endure the anxiety and resist using escape procedures. The counselor will remind the student that resistance to engage in escape or ritualistic behavior will allow the anxiety to begin to decrease by itself. As the session continues, the student will remain in the exposure, refraining from the previous coping strategies, until the anxiety decreases 60 percent—80 percent, or to a SUDS score of 20 or less. This exposure will be repeated as many times as feasible, or until the initial anxiety level remains consistently low; this repetition functions both (a) as a model for homework exercises and (b) to illustrate the relative reduction in anxiety over successive exposures. It is important that the first exposure exercise ends with positive results and all exposures are repeated until response prevention is maintained. Typically, counselors employing this approach will assign one to two hours of homework for the student to complete prior to the next session. The assignment selected will provide the student with a form of exposure that will most likely be successful in producing an experience without employing their coping response. This homework reinforces the value of this approach while facilitating the habituation to the feared stimuli and rapid attenuation of distress.

Subsequent sessions will review the homework and identify the degree to which the homework was successful. If the student did not do the homework, barriers need to be identified and strategies employed to assist in future homework completion. Even under these conditions, the student's attempts should be praised. Each session will then return to the hierarchy starting at the last successful step and gradually continue up the hierarchy.

When the specific form of stimulus is hard to produce or manage within the session, as would be the case with a student who is afraid of her house catching on fire, the counselor and student may employ "imaginable exposure." Imaginable exposure involves exposing the person to situations that trigger anxiety by imagining different scenes. In general, the more detailed and horrifying the imagined scene employed, the more successful the procedure.

Step 4. Providing Support and Encouragement

Since the main goal during both in vivo and imaginable exposure is for the person to stay in contact with the anxiety trigger, while resisting engaging in the ritual anxiety-reducing behavior, it is important for the counselor to encourage the student to endure the initial discomfort, sitting with it until the anxiety dissipates. In session, the counselor will encourage the student to stay with the image—or the engagement with the fear stimuli—and not employ any form of distraction or avoidance techniques, since these will prevent habituation. Michelle, for example, would be supported and encouraged to resist her desire to engage in her repetitive hand-washing behavior. Initially, she may be asked to resist for a couple of hours and eventually increase her resistance until she can abstain from the ritual activities altogether. Progress in exposure therapy is often slow in the beginning, and occasional setbacks are to be expected. As the student gains experience with various anxiety-producing situations, his or her rate of progress may increase.

PUNISHMENT

For many school personnel, efforts to reduce or eliminate undesirable behavior involve application of "punishments," such as detentions, demerits, and in- and out-of-school suspensions. The use of punishment is not without its controversy, and clearly no humane person or caring professional would endorse procedures that are dehumanizing, socially degrading, or physically harmful. But, in situations where the student's behavior places him or her in great danger or serious harm, as would be the case with a developmentally disabled student who is at risk of damaging her hearing by clapping her hands against her ears with such force as to tear the flesh and cause bleeding, punishment may be an effective intervention (see Linscheid, Pejeau, Cohen, & Footo-Lenz, 1994).

The fundamental principle underlying the use of punishers is that if, in a given situation, the behavior which the student manifests is followed by an undesirable consequence, then the student will be less likely to engage in that same behavior when encountering similar situations in the future. However, it is *essential* to remember a punishment like a reinforcement is known only as it functions. For some students, an out of school suspension is a welcomed vacation and, as such, serves to strengthen the behavior that resulted in the suspension. A punisher is defined by how the event operates. If an event following a behavior results in that behavior's reduction in frequency, then we can assume the event was a punisher.

It is important to understand a couple of subtle differences between this use of the term "punisher" and the more typical examples of punishment. From a behavioral perspective, a punisher is a contingency applied immediately following the targeted behavior, which has as its sole intent the reduction of this specific behavior within this specific situation. If one contrasts this definition to the more secular use of the word "punishment," as when applied to the process of incarceration, for example, we recognize that the imprisonment is not an event immediately following the undesirable behavior. It is often employed for purposes of eliciting a modeling, preventive effect for other possible lawbreakers and to extract retribution from the lawbreaker. For school counselors operating with a behavioral orientation, the application of "punishers" and punishment is viewed not as retribution or social statements, but rather an intervention intended to reduce the likelihood of the occurrence of this specific, undesirable behavior.

The fundamental nature of a behavioral punisher is that it is an event highlighting that a certain behavior will result in an unpleasant consequence. Consider, for example, the experience of touching a hot stove. When touching a hot stove, not only do we respond to the intense stimuli by rapidly withdrawing our hand, but we "learn" to reduce the likelihood of repeating that behavior (i.e., touching a hot stove). In most cases, we don't feel like a bad person, nor do we necessarily "hate" the stove and feel it has delivered an injustice to us. Rather, we accept that there were signals that we failed to recognize, that would have warned us that a certain behavior (i.e., touching the burner) would have resulted in a noxious experience. We will be more alert to these signals and most likely choose not to repeat the behavior when it is clear the same experience will be incurred.

Types of Punishers

Van Houten (1983) categorized "punishers" as: (a) physical, (b) reprimand, (c) time-out, and (d) response costs. For counselors working within the school setting, both as direct service providers and consultants to others, such as parents and teachers, the use of time-out and response costs appear to be valid tools to have in their counseling tool boxes.

Time-Out

Time-out (TO) is one of the most frequently researched and widely applied behavior management techniques. Time-out is conceptualized as time away from reinforcing events (Jones & Downing, 1991). Time-out is a process whereby a student exhibiting an undesirable behavior is removed from a situation in which reinforcement is available (Carter, 1994).

This would be the situation when a student who acts out in group in order to gain peer attention is removed from group and thus the availability of gaining this desired attention. For the procedure to be effective, the duration of time-out in a less reinforcing environment must be made contingent on the occurrence of a target behavior. Also, there must be a functional difference between the availability of reinforcement in the natural and TO environments.

Considerable research suggests that time-out successfully reduces a variety of student behavior problems, including noncompliance, disruptive behavior, and tantrums (Everett, Olmi, Edwards, Tingstrom, Sterling-Turner, & Christ, 2007; Reavis, Sweeten, Jenson, Morgan, Andrews, & Fister, 1996; Walker, 1995). It has also been shown that TO is effective across a wide range of settings with children of varying ages and functioning levels. However, TO is a technique that has been misused and can be ineffective, even counterproductive. When ineffective as a treatment it is often because of the inappropriate timing, the inconsistent use, or simply the ineffective level or duration of the time-out. Table 4.1 provides a number of recommendations that should be used as guidelines when considering time-out as an intervention strategy.

Table 4.1   Guidelines for Using Time-Out (TO)

1. Student needs to understand why he or she is being removed from the situation.

2. Those imposing the time-out (teacher, parent, counselor) need to be clear that the student is being removed from a reinforcing situation, rather than using the misbehavior to simply escape an undesirable situation.

3. Time-out area needs to be safe and humane—no closets, cardboard boxes, etc.

4. Time-out area should not be reinforcing.

5. Time-out should not be used for extended period . . . in general, no more than fifteen minutes with opportunity to regain access and admission to the desired environment.

Time-out cannot be used to exclude a child from education, thus cannot be used so frequently or for such lengths of time as to restrict the child access to education.

Response Cost

Pfiffner and O'Leary (1987), in assessing the effectiveness of various behavioral interventions, found that the combination of positive and negative consequences was most effective in improving student on-task behavior and academic performance. One strategy, often used in tangent with positive reinforcement for appropriate behavior, is the loss of privileges as consequence for inappropriate behaviors (Fiore, Becker, & Nero, 1993). This process, known as *response cost*, has been shown to lead to greater improvements in on-task rates, academic accuracy, and greater maintenance of treatment effects following termination of treatment (Carlson, Mann, & Alexander, 2000), when compared to the use of reinforcement alone.

Response-cost procedures involve the removal of pre-established reinforcements as a contingency on engaging in undesirable behavior. A typical application of response cost would be the situation where the student earns tokens for the performance of targeted behaviors, for example, waiting to be recognized in group prior to speaking, but then also has tokens deducted contingent upon inappropriate behavior, which in this scenario may be behaviors such as yelling out or talking over another group member who has been given the floor. Table 4.2 provides a number of guidelines to consider when employing response-cost procedures.

Table 4.2   Guidelines for Using Response Cost

1. It is important to use response cost only for severe offenses.

2. Do not overpenalize a student. This may elicit anger and resistance to continue in the program.

3. Just as amount of tokens to be distributed by the performance of a desired behavior is clearly identified and explained to the student, the specific number of tokens that misbehavior "costs" needs to be concretely defined and explained.

4. If a student "resists" or in some way misbehaves in response to having tokens removed, this resistance should also be penalized.

5. It is important to be alert to "catch the student being good" following a response cost, so that they can experience reinforcement as soon as possible following the response cost implementation.

The Use of Punishment: Some Caveats and Considerations

Punishment has been shown to be effective in suppressing undesirable behavior, allowing for the opportunity to differentially reinforce an acceptable alternative behavior. However, the use of punishment can result in potentially harmful effects, and thus should be used only after careful consideration of all the limitations to punishment as an intervention strategy.

1. Perhaps the biggest limitation is that punishment *does not* establish any new behavior; it only suppresses the undesirable behavior. As noted above, the suppressive effect, when combined with differential reinforcement can be a value intervention. However, punishment when applied to individuals who fail to have the desired alternative behavior within their repertoire will be ineffective, and in these cases shaping and the employment of reinforcement would be more desirable.

2. Punishment may elicit aggressive behaviors.

3. It is possible for the aversive effects of punishment to become associated with the person (i.e., teacher, counselor, parent) and the situation (i.e., counselor's office or classroom), thus making these individuals and situations conditioned punishers. Thus, while the student may initially seek to escape or avoid the punishment, that escape and avoidance behavior may be generalized to the individual or situation associated with the punishment.

Adults employing punishment as a method of behavioral intervention also model this strategy. Thus, it is possible that the student, or those observing the process, may "learn" to use punishment as a strategy to be employed with their peers.

SUMMARY

Extinction

- Extinction of operant behavior involves the termination of the reinforcement contingency that maintains the response.
- Extinction by omission requires that all reinforcement in response to the student's misbehavior is removed.
- Noncontingent reinforcement is a form of extinction that is based on the principle that inappropriate behavior has proven effective in acquiring some desirable consequence, such as experiencing that consequence irrespective of the behavior will break the link between the inappropriate behavior and the desired consequence.

- Extinction procedures should never be used if the student is in real physical distress, in harm's way, may be a danger to others, or when the environmental situation just isn't conducive to this technique.
- When considering the use of extinction, the counselor needs to be aware that the behavior could initially get worse (extinction bump).

Differential Reinforcement

- If we attempt to eliminate a behavior without attending to the purpose it served, we may find that the behavior reappears or another behavior, perhaps one even less desirable, may take its place in order to achieve the same end.
- When planning on removing these behaviors, it is helpful to simultaneously plan on developing an alternative, more desirable behavior that will serve a similar function.
- Differential reinforcement involves the extinction of the undesired behavior along with the simultaneous reinforcement of a differential and appropriate response.

Flooding

- The key to this procedure is the rapid, condensed exposure to the troublesome stimuli or situation.
- This concentrated experience of the previously associated fear situation *in the absence* of real pain or harmful outcome results in a reduction of the fear response.

Exposure and Response Prevention (ERP)

- ERP is predicated on the belief that anxiety can be reduced or extinguished if the student is confronted by his or her fear stimuli and prevented from escaping from the situation under a condition where there is no accompanying pain or danger.
- The "exposure" part of this treatment involves either direct or imagined controlled exposure to objects or situations that trigger the anxiety. Over time, exposure to these objects or situations leads to less and less anxiety.
- For this reduction to occur, the student cannot escape or avoid the exposure. Thus, the second part of the process is the

(Continued)

(Continued)

"response prevention." The "response" in "response prevention" refers to the repetitive and often ritualized behaviors employed by the student to escape and/or avoid the anxiety.

Punishment

- From a behavioral perspective, a punisher is a contingency applied immediately following the targeted behavior and has as its sole intent the reduction of this specific behavior within this specific situation.
- Punishers could include: (a) physical, (b) reprimand, (c) time-out, and (d) response costs.
- Punishment has been shown to be effective in suppressing undesirable behavior, allowing for the opportunity to differentially reinforce an acceptable alternative behavior. However, the use of punishment can result in potentially harmful effects, and thus should be used only after careful consideration of all the limitations to punishment as an intervention strategy.

Counterconditioning 5

Counterconditioning is the process by which a response to a particular stimuli is now replaced with a new—incompatible—response. This new response, once established, serves to counteract the previous tendency to engage in the identified behavior of concern. For example, a person who previously felt positively toward smoking but now wants to avoid such behavior may be taught to associate negative feelings with the act of smoking. If this connection occurs, cigarettes would elicit an avoidance response and thus the act of smoking would be eliminated. Or, consider a person who has learned to become anxious in certain social situations, for example, while making a class presentation; counterconditioning would teach this person to associate positive, pleasant experience in that same setting—thus counteracting the previously learned anxiety response. In both cases, the processes employed would be those of counterconditioning and both are based on the principles of respondent learning.

A BRIEF REVIEW OF RESPONDENT CONDITIONING

Counterconditioning employs the fundamental paradigm previously articulated by Ivan Pavlov and identified as respondent conditioning. In this paradigm, two stimuli are paired together in time and space in such a manner that they become associated and thus share characteristics. In the classic study of respondent conditioning, a dog is presented with meat powder, which by nature appeared to elicit a salivation response. Since this response was a natural response—one not needing to be learned—it was termed an *unconditioned* (i.e., unlearned) *response* (UCR) and the meat powder, which served as the "natural" eliciting stimuli, was labeled the *unconditioned stimuli* (UCS). Now, in this presentation (see Figure 5.1), the meat powder (i.e., UCS) was paired with a neutral signal—neutral in that it did not automatically elicit a salivation response. The pairing was repeated until the neutral signal (i.e., bell) took on the eliciting power of the meat powder and the dog responded with salivation to the sound of the bell. This new behavior, salivating to the sound of the bell, was learned. That is, a *conditioned response* (CR) and the meat in this situation now became a *conditioned stimuli* (CS), or one to which the animal learned to respond.

Figure 5.1 Respondent Conditioning

Before Conditioning	Conditioning
Food Powder → Salivation	*Pairing UCS and UCR*
(UCS) (UCR)	Food Powder → Salivation
	(UCS) (UCR)
Bell → Orientation but No Salivation	↕
(neutral)	Bell → Salivation as Learned (CS)
	(CR)

This paradigm has been employed to teach individuals to have negative reactions in the presence of specific stimuli (e.g., cigarettes, alcohol) with the aim for clients to experience aversion to what has now become noxious stimuli. While this use of counterconditioning known as *aversive therapy* may be appropriate and useful for clinical settings, it does not appear to be one that a school counselor would necessarily employ. However, a second technique that employs counterconditioning and which a school counselor may find useful is *systematic desensitization*. Systematic desensitization is a procedure found to be very useful in helping students combat debilitating anxiety.

SYSTEMATIC DESENSITIZATION

Consider the situation in which a student, who while academically talented, now struggles in her advanced placement class because of the requirement to make formal presentations in front of the class. In talking with her school counselor, the student explains that she finds herself becoming preoccupied with worrisome thoughts each time she enters this class. She even notes that as the day of her presentation draws closer she finds that she is getting sick to her stomach and feeling as if she is going to panic. Clearly, her level of anxiety is debilitating to her academic performance and simply making school, or at least this class, something less than enjoyable.

In this situation, as with most performance anxiety, the reaction to the "anticipated danger" of the event is disproportionate to the actual threat value of that situation. While exposure to the feared situation (i.e., class presentation) in the absence of real harm or pain may be the most expedient way to reduce this fear (as cited by Smith & Glass in Wierzbicki, 1999), this student may be unable to attend to the realities of the experience (that it is nonharmful or painful) and rather be absorbed in her own experience of anxiety. When the level of anxiety is such that the student will simply refuse to place him- or herself in the presence of the feared item, or once experiencing the stimuli finds that he or she cannot remain in that situation, a graduated presentation of the feared stimuli may prove more useful.

Systematic desensitization employs this graduated presentation of the feared stimuli and has extensive support demonstrating its efficacy (Barrios & O'Dell, 1998; King & Ollendick, 1998). Desensitization employs counter-conditioning to teach the student a new response to the feared stimuli, a response that proves incompatible with and thus inhibitory of the previously learned anxiety response. As noted by Wolpe (1958), this learned anxiety will be weakened and thus alleviated if "[. . .] a response antagonistic to anxiety can be made to occur in the presence of anxiety–evoking stimuli so that it is accompanied by a complete or partial suppression of the anxiety responses" (p. 71). For example, a preschool child who has developed the habit of crying when his parents leave the classroom may be taught not to cry by pairing the experience of having his parents leave the classroom with a stimulus that causes him to laugh (see Figure 5.2). The key, of course, is for the antagonistic response (e.g., laughing) to be stronger than the anxiety produced by the event.

Figure 5.2   Counterconditioning

Current Conditioned Response	**Antagonistic Response**
Parents leave → Anxiety	Playing with toy → Happy/relaxed

Counterconditioning

Parents separate
while child   Anxiety
plays with   →   neutralized
favorite toy.   by happiness

Systematic desensitization appears to be a treatment of choice when: (1) anxiety is elicited in the absence of objective danger or threat of real harm, (2) the response pattern of anxiety is causing disruption to adaptive functioning, and (3) maladaptive behaviors have been learned and main-tained to alleviate or avoid anxiety. Thus, returning to the example of our advanced-placement student, clearly the presentation of material in front of her peers will not result in real harm; further, the level of her anxiety is causing her physical discomfort and now she finds that she is avoiding thinking about the presentation and thus not truly preparing for it. Under these conditions, she would appear to be a prime candidate for systematic desensitization.

THE SYSTEMATIC DESENSITIZATION PACKAGE

As implied by its title, this intervention is clearly *systematic* and requires the full engagement of the counselor and the student in the development and implementation of the intervention plan. For the school counselor employing systematic desensitization, the role to be played and the tasks to be accomplished are clearly identified. As with all counseling, prior to the employment of such an intervention, the school counselor needs to establish rapport, assess the nature and basis of the student's problems, and certainly explain and engage the student's full cooperation. Assuming these fundamentals are established, the counselor will first invite the student to identify the specific conditions, or stimuli, that elicit the anxiety experience. Thus, for example, a school counselor may engage with students who experience disruptive anxiety when placed in peer-social situations, or when required to stand before the class to make a presentation, or even when confronted with a standardized test.

Once the general area of concern is identified, the work of identifying the various specific elements and stimuli involved in the situation begins. The counselor and student review the situations in order to identify specific stimuli that will be used in the desensitization process. Thus, the student who is overwhelmed with anxiety when required to make a class presentation may identify stimuli that contribute to the anxiety experience as: (1) walking up to the front of the class, (2) standing at the podium, (3) seeing the classmates looking at her, (4) seeing the teacher in the back of the room taking notes, (5) hearing her voice as she begins to speak, etc. The third task is to make sure that the student has developed and can employ an anxiety-inhibiting response. This step may require that the counselor actually teach the student an anxiety-inhibiting response, such as deep muscle relaxation. The fourth task is for the counselor to present those stimuli that will elicit anxiety in such a manner (i.e., hierarchical fashion) that they will never produce an anxiety response at a level of intensity greater than the antagonistic response being used. It is this graduated presentation of these anxiety-eliciting stimuli in a sequence of increasing intensity that is the hallmark of systematic desensitization.

There are numerous variations in the above application. The treatment is typically employed once or twice a week for thirty to forty minute sessions. What follows is a "generic" outline and description of the elements in the systematic desensitization process. However, it must be highlighted that nuance and subtle adjustments should be considered in order to tailor the procedures to each specific student.

Constructing and Scaling Items for Hierarchy

Since the intent is to pair an anxiety-eliciting stimulus with an experience, for example relaxation, which inhibits that anxiety, it is *essential* that the amount of anxiety elicited by the provoking stimuli is less than the degree of anxiety inhibition induced or produced by way of the relaxation practice. To insure that is the case, the counselor and student need to develop an anxiety hierarchy.

Anxiety hierarchies are simply graded lists of stimuli that the student believes or has evidence of eliciting anxiety reactions. In the ideal, the hierarchy is constructed to include items that elicit equal units of noticeable difference in felt anxiety. There is no attempt to make an objective, quantitative listing of increasing intensity—rather, it is the student's subjective experience that guides the ordering of stimuli or situations from the least anxiety provoking to the most. It is important that the items included in the hierarchy are real representations of the situations that elicit the anxiety response and the type that the student may face in the future. This will require that the counselor and student explore in depth the details of these anxiety-provoking events and that the counselor employ the actual descriptions and language provided by the student in the development of the hierarchy.

Types of Hierarchies

Hierarchies are generally one of two types—thematic or spatial-temporal. *Thematic hierarchies* are focused about some "cluster" of anxiety-eliciting stimuli or stimulus configurations. For example, a hierarchy could be established around the "theme" of rejection, criticism, death . . . or even driving a car. Figure 5.3 provides a sample thematic hierarchy, where theme is "driving alone."

Figure 5.3   Thematic Hierarchy: Driving a Car Alone

1. Sit in the garaged car for five minutes, alone.
2. Start the car in the driveway and sit while car is running for five minutes.
3. Drive to the first stop sign, one block, and come to smooth stop.
4. Drive around the block making right turns.
5. Drive through the neighborhood making right and left turns.
6. Drive on a minor artery, right lane only.
7. Drive on a minor artery, crossing over to middle lane to make left turn.
8. Drive a major artery during traffic.
9. Drive a major artery and change lanes to make a left turn.
10. Drive on the turnpike or freeway, changing lanes and passing cars for one mile.

Thematic hierarchies are sometimes more difficult to construct since they can involve multiple factors or parameters. As suggested in our illustration (see Figure 5.3), driving alone could be impacted by issues of speed, amount of traffic, type of road, etc. Thus, it may be important at first to desensitize the student to each of these issues, and then the terminal point at the top-most portion of the hierarchy would be scenarios that include all possible interactions of factors.

Spatial-temporal hierarchies address target events that are located in a particular time and space with the hierarchy reflecting points along an approach continuum. Thus, one hierarchy that could be developed for a student experiencing anxiety when giving a class presentation would be based on the amount of time remaining before delivering a speech (temporal) (see Figure 5.4). A spatial hierarchy may be employed in situations where physical proximity to an item causes anxiety. For example, consider a counselor who attempts to reduce the degree of anxiety experienced by an elementary-school student when in the presence of a class pet gerbil. In this case, the hierarchy would be created based on distance between the student and proximity to the gerbil.

Figure 5.4 Temporal Hierarchy: Class Presentation

1. Two weeks prior to presentation, create outline for speech.
2. Ten days prior to presentation, develop text.
3. One week prior to presentation, practice in front of the mirror.
4. Three days prior to presentation, practice in front of parents.
5. One day prior to presentation, practice in the classroom after school.
6. On the day of the presentation, rehearse during study hall (two classes removed).
7. On the day of presentation, go over speech cards during lunch (period prior to presentation).
8. Sitting in class, listen to first student of the day, with three to present and I'm the last presenter.
9. Sitting in class, listen the second student of the day present.
10. Sitting in class, listen to the second student state "in conclusion" and wrap up the presentation.
11. Sitting in class, listen to classmates applaud the end of the second presentation.
12. Sitting in class, listen to teacher thank student for the presentation and begin to announce the last presenter of the day (me).
13. Hear my name called to come to front of the class.
14. Walk to the podium.
15. Turn at podium and see my classmates.
16. Begin to speak and hear my voice.

Regardless of the focus or type of hierarchy, the actual construction is extremely reliant on the student's active involvement. The student plays an essential role in the construction process. Not only does the student present the general situations and then the detailed elements, but also serves to arrange these items in order of increasing anxiety. The goal—which the counselor needs to facilitate—is to establish a relatively, evenly spaced set of items along the anxiety continuum.

Scaling

A number of different methods have been employed to scale the varying levels of anxiety that elicit power among the items on the hierarchy. These include rank-ordering, subjective unit of discomfort scale (SUDS), and equal-appearing intervals.

Rank Ordering

A relatively simple, yet highly subjective, scaling procedure is one in which the counselor and student identify anxiety arousing situations and place these on 3 × 5-index cards. These cards are laid out and arranged in order of increasing anxiety. By manipulating the cards, items can be arranged and placed. Gaps where the interval is too large can be identified and additional situations created to fill that gap.

"SUDS" Scaling

In this procedure, introduced in the previous chapter, items are arranged on a 100–point "subjective units of discomfort" scale (SUDS). On this scale, 100 SUDS would reflect situations in which there is uncontrollable anxiety and 0 would indicate situations of complete relaxation. Using this process, the counselor and student attempt to identify items that would fit at all points along the scale. It is not necessary that the counselor and student identify 100 items to correspond to each point along the scale, but as a general rule, it is important to find stimuli or experiences which could be placed at least at each 5-point interval.

Equal-Appearing Intervals

A third approach often used is for the counselor and student to decide on an arbitrary number of steps to be included in the hierarchy, for example, fifteen steps. The student would be asked to identify the worst-case scenario or situation he or she can imagine and this is placed at the top of the hierarchy. The counselor then attempts to help the student identify a situation that would arouse minimal anxiety. Once these end points are established, the counselor and student attempt to identify situations that fit midway between these two extremes. With this as a new reference point, the counselor and student attempt to identify a situation that would be midpoint between this center point and the lowest, as well as one that would fit between this center point and the highest. This process of "mid-pointing" continues until all steps have illustrative scenarios or stimuli associated with them.

Developing Anxiety Inhibiting Responses: Relaxation Training

As noted previously, a key element in this process of desensitization is the student's ability to respond to the identified stimuli in a manner that is antagonistic to anxiety. It is this antagonistic response that results in the inhibition of the anxiety. It is important for the school counselor to appreciate that instructing the student to "simply relax," or "take a deep breath" may be insufficient. If these were responses the student could easily employ in the situations that currently evoke anxiety, the student would not be anxious. Thus, it is important for the counselor to spend time "teaching" the student how to employ the anxiety-inhibiting response, which will be used in the desensitization process.

While there are many techniques that have been employed in teaching a student to relax—including deep breathing and imagery—the most typical form of relaxation training involves systematic muscle relaxation. It is a method the most students can learn in a relatively short period of time and is easy to employ within the counselor's office, classroom, or home environments.

The method continuing today to be the most widely used is that originally detailed by Jacobson (1938) and termed progressive relaxation. While most often employed in modified and abbreviated form such as that presented in Figure 5.5, the technique starts with teaching the student to relax by successively tensing and then releasing gross muscle groups throughout the body. The student's attention is focused upon identification of points of stress and tension, as well as the resulting change in experience as the tension is let go.

Figure 5.5   Directing Deep Muscle Relaxation

Rationale (presented to student)

When you feel tense, upset, or nervous, certain muscles in your body tighten. If you could learn to identify these muscles and relax them, then any time these muscles are tense in different situations, you could relax the muscles and feel the opposite of being tense. You'll have to feel relaxed because the muscles are relaxed.

What we are going to do is practice tensing these muscles and then relaxing them. This will help you learn to identify the muscles that are tight when you are nervous, and then use the skills that you will learn to relax them. If you learn to relax the way you have been taught and you practice, then after a while, you'll be able to relax in a situation where you feel anxious. Also, if you are going into a situation in which you feel you are going to be tense, then you can relax just before you go into that situation. If you have just been in a situation that made you upset or anxious and it still bothers you, then you can relax and minimize the effect on you.

Phase I: Tensing-Relaxing

Tense

Sit in a chair and keep your head squarely on your shoulders, not bending it forward or backward. Keep your legs uncrossed and feet flat on the floor. Put your hands on your thighs. Now just generally try to relax.

The procedure to be used will be a series of tensing specific muscles, holding that tension, and then letting go and relaxing. You will be asked to focus on the specific muscles and how they feel when tensed, and then after relaxing, notice the change in experience. So the sequence will be: (1) tense and hold for ten seconds, (2) scan, (3) relax, (4) enjoy the pleasant feeling, and (5) repeat sequence for that muscle group.

Target Muscle Groups

Forehead. Wrinkle your forehead. Notice where it feels particularly tense (over the bridge of the nose and above each eyebrow). Slowly relax your forehead, and pay special attention to those areas that are particularly tense. Notice how it feels to have those muscles loosen, switch off, and relax.

Eyes. Close your eyes very tightly, and really squeeze them. (They should feel tense above and below each eyelid and the peripheries.) Gradually open your eyes and notice the difference in the way they feel. *(Caution: be sure the student is not wearing contacts or if so skip this target area.)*

Nose. Wrinkle your nose. (Tense areas are the bridge and nostrils.)

Smile. Put your face in a forced smile (upper and lower lips and cheeks on each side).

Tongue. Put your tongue hard against the roof of your mouth (include inside of mouth and tongue, and muscles just below jaws).

Teeth-Jaws. Clinch your teeth (besides the muscles on side of face, also include temples).

Lips. Pucker your lips (upper and lower lips and sides of lips).

Neck. Tighten your neck (Adam's apple and on each side, also back of neck).

(Continued)

Figure 5.5 (Continued)

Arms. Put your right arm out straight, make a fist, and tighten your whole arm from hand to your shoulder (biceps, forearm, back of arm, elbow above and below wrist, and fingers). Repeat with left arm.

Legs. As you did with your arms, extend your right leg and tighten all of the muscles involved—the hamstring, and quads—squeeze your calf and hold. Let go and repeat with left leg.

Core. Crunch your stomach muscles as hard as you can.

Relax

Now, close your eyes and try to relax your whole body. Notice any part that is tense and try to relax it. Take a deep breath, hold it, and then exhale slowly. While you are exhaling, try to get your body relaxed from head to toes. It's like someone waving a magic wand in front of you starting at your head and going down toward your toes. As the wand goes down, your body gets relaxed when the wand passes. Do this five times, and then breathe the same way again, except this time, as you start to exhale, mentally say the word "relax." Drag it out slowly so that as you reach the "x" of the word "relax" you are down to your toes. Do five of these.

Phase II: Relaxing Without Tensing

After you have become familiar and comfortable with the muscle tensing-relaxing process, you will now practice trying to relax the muscles, without first tensing them. You do not have to tense any part unless you have trouble relaxing it. Go through each part and relax it as well as you can. After all the parts have been done, do five deep breathing exercises while mentally repeating the word "relax."

It is very important that you practice. It's like every other skill; the more you practice the better you'll be at it. You should practice the two phases (tensing-relaxing and relaxing without tensing) twice a day. Therefore, your practice sessions will consist of tensing each part, noting where it is tense and relaxing it gradually, and noting the muscles that are relaxing. After you have done this, do all the parts again without tensing anything, but concentrating on each part. Then take ten more deep breaths. Initially, this will take fifteen–twenty minutes each day. Eventually you will be able to do just the second part—relaxing without tensing, with deep breathing.

After you can achieve relaxation by doing just the second part, you should practice relaxation while standing, and then while walking. That is, when you are standing, like while you wait in a line, concentrate on each part and relax it, and take smooth, rhythmic breaths. Even when you are walking, scan each muscle group, relax it, and engage in smooth, rhythmic breathing.

While Figure 5.5 provides a sequence and set of verbal instruction to use, it is important to realize that the sequence and combination of muscles can be varied depending on the time available and the student's resources. Some students, for example, may find it difficult to tense a specific muscle so it is acceptable to simply move on to another group.

In addition to teaching this progressive muscle technique, it is useful to help students develop a breathing rhythm that similarly contributes to creation of relaxation. Typically, when experiencing stress and anxiety, our breathing becomes shallow, rapid, and often somewhat sporadic. If we envision a child who is upset, we could take note of the staccato-type rhythm of his or her shallow, rapid breathing. Contrast this to the smooth, slow, rhythmic breathing of a child at rest and we have a good illustration of what has been termed as the quieting response. Figure 5.6 provides a set of simple instructions when teaching the quieting response. It is helpful to record these instructions using a pleasant, calm, soothing voice and invite the student to practice by listening to the tape at home.

Figure 5.6   Deep Breathing: The Quieting Response

Instructions: The following simple steps will help you to employ slow, smooth, and rhythmic breathing as a means to experience relaxation. Practice the following a few minutes each day.

1. Find a comfortable seat to relax in and place your hands firmly on your stomach.

2. Inhale slowly and deeply through your nose, allowing your stomach to expand as much as possible.

3. After inhaling deeply, allow the inhaling to simply pause at its peak. Do not hold your breath for an extended time, but rather, simply allow it to pause as it reverses in the process of exhaling. Perhaps it would help to envision a swing at its highest point that seems momentarily suspended—or paused—in mid-air and then reverses its direction. That is the rhythm to be established for your breathing . . . in . . . pause . . . out . . . pause . . . in . . .

4. Keeping your hands on your stomach to monitor your breathing, exhale slowly through your mouth. Keep the pace slow yet rhythmic. You want to establish a slow, comfortable, and smooth in-breath and a pause followed by a similarly slow, comfortable, and smooth out-breath.

5. Repeat the process, and now, while exhaling, think to yourself the word "relax" as you exhale and continue the process, focusing on gaining slow . . . smooth . . . rhythmic breathing.

PUTTING IT ALL TOGETHER: THE PROCESS

Once the hierarchy has been established and the student is able to employ a relaxation response, the actual system of desensitization can begin.

Setting the Stage

It's important for the counselor to redescribe the process to be employed and to answer any questions the student may have. It is also important to highlight or reiterate the essential role played by the student. The student needs to focus and be attentive to levels of increased anxiety. It is important that he or she signals when anxiety increases beyond a predetermined level. For example, if during the scene presentation, the student begins to experience anxiety at a SUDS level of 10, the counselor would want the student to stop imagining that item, refocus on the relaxation, and perhaps return to a lower item on the scale. The student could be instructed, "When you feel yourself becoming anxious, just raise your right index finger. Then switch off the scene you have been imagining, and return to your relaxation image and breathing. Continue relaxation until I suggest we focus on a particular scene."

Using Imagery

The student will be reminded that the items on the hierarchy will be presented in detail and his or her task is to create and maintain a clear visual image of that scenario. The scenes presented should be described in detail, with all visual, auditory, and even olfactory and tactile components included. Thus, for the counselor working with the student with "presentation anxiety," the scene may be:

> *You are sitting at your desk and the current student-presenter is just finishing. The room is filled with all of your classmates. The teacher is sitting right off the side of the podium. The podium is dead center in the front of the room. The room is a bit warm and the students are some-what fidgety in their seats. Some are looking at their notebooks, others apparently daydreaming but most clearly focused on the speaker at the front of the room. You know that you are next on the list to present. You hear the student presenter say, "thank you very much," and the students in the class begin to clap. You see the student standing there— you hear the clapping—you see the teacher looking at the list of student presenters and you know that your name is the one he will identify as next to present. Keep this image in your mind . . . hold it . . . focus on the details . . . the teacher in the front, the podium, your classmates staring at the student-presenter. Keep focusing but remain relaxed, using your calm breathing. Hold that image . . . hold it!*

Presenting the Scene

As presented in the brief illustration, the counselor, starting with the lowest item on the hierarchy, and after the student has placed him- or herself in a relaxed state, will briefly but vividly describe the scenario for the student to visualize. If the counselor uses a live "in vivo" presentation of the feared item, rather than employing imagery, the items in the hierarchy would be presented physically. For example, in the case of our elementary student afraid of the class pet, a "cartoon sketch of a gerbil" may be the lowest item on the hierarchy that would be physically handed to the student. The student would be asked to focus—consider and experience the item in the presence of the relaxed state. Exposure to the image or the actual item should be for approximately twenty seconds, at which time the student is instructed to "turn off" the image, or if using a live presentation, to close their eyes and return to the process of relaxing and stay with that experience of relaxation for about a minute. Assuming success at this level, the item would be reintroduced. Each item on the hierarchy should be presented and successfully encountered while the student is able to remain calm, before proceeding to the next item on the hierarchy. The process continues until all items of the hierarchy have been presented and experienced while remaining calm, moving from the lowest to the highest.

Special Considerations

1. Each session should end with a "successful" item presentation. Thus, if the student has difficulty relaxing with one item on the hierarchy, the counselor will return to the next lowest item, and reintroduce this stimulus as a means of reinforcing the success of the process. If in future sessions the student continues to have difficulty moving from the success item to the next highest item, the counselor and student need to revisit the hierarchy and add additional steps. Subsequent sessions would begin where the previous session terminated—at a point of success.

2. Scene presentations, as noted, are typically for a period of twenty seconds, and a period of usually thirty to sixty seconds of relaxation is employed between item presentations. However, if a student has difficulty returning to relaxed state within a minute or two, this may be an indication that additional steps in the hierarchy need to be developed or the relaxation process needs further practice.

3. Typically, sessions may last ten to thirty minutes and are scheduled twice or sometimes three times a week. In the extreme, the student should at least continue in the process once a week. The short, yet frequent sessions which have been found most successful for systematic desensitization also appear quite in line with the typical time available for school counselors' counseling sessions.

4. The process described here highlighted the employment of imagery presentation of feared stimuli. This is the more "classic" approach to systematic desensitization, but it has been adapted to include actual live, in-vivo presentations of the stimuli that elicited an anxiety response. Clearly, this approach is limited by the actual availability of these feared items and the appropriateness of their utilization within a school setting. Readers interested in a more detailed discussion of in-vivo presentation with children should refer to MacPhee and Andrews (2003).

We close this chapter with a brief look at a counselor's adjustment in session while working with Matt, a student experiencing anxiety when asked to speak publicly within the classroom (Case Illustration 5.1)

Case Illustration 5.1   Matt: Fear of Public Speaking

Session One: Describing the Scenario

Counselor: So if I understand, you were in class and you began to feel your heart beating and felt like your stomach was going to leap out of your throat. This was happening right as you were called to present your report in social studies?

Matt: Yeah, it was unbelievable . . . I was sweating, thought I would pass out.

Counselor: I'm sure that was really uncomfortable. If we were grading the degree of anxiety that you were feeling at that time, on scale where 0 equaled absolutely no anxiety and 100 was the most anxiety you have ever experienced, where would this scene of the social-science report be?

Matt: It was really bad—maybe a 60 or 70!

Counselor: Could you describe what was going on at the time? What you remember you saw, or heard, in as much detail as possible?

Matt: Well, Mrs. Federico called my name to come up to the front and I can remember standing up from my desk and walking past my pal, Jeremy. He whispered, "Lots of luck." I got to the front of the class and turned around at the podium. I saw Liz, my friend, staring at me. She looked really worried for me.

Counselor: So here's what I wrote—tell me if this reminds you of that specific event! "I heard Mrs. Federico call my name and I got up, walked past Jeremy who was smiling and said, 'lots of luck' and when I turned to see the class I saw Liz—staring at me!"

Matt: Yeah, that's it. Gads, my stomach is in a knot just talking about it.

Session Two: Constructing Matt's Fear Hierarchy

Being called up to the front of senior assembly and singing the national anthem.	100
Having to sing a solo in music class when I am required to sight-read the music.	90
Practicing my Christmas solo in front of my music class.	80
Providing an oral report in class with Liz (the girl I like) staring at me.	70
As president of the student government, introducing the principal at student assemblies.	60
Being on stage as part of the student government when the students are invited to observe one of our meetings.	50
Participating in a mock debate in social studies class as a member of the "affirmative" team.	40
Practicing my social studies speech in front of my mom and dad.	30
Having my mom listen to my Christmas solo.	20
Presenting the sales script that I use in my part-time job as a telephone solicitor.	10

Session Three: Employing Desensitization With Scene at SUDS 50

Counselor: So, here you are; you are walking up on the stage for the student government meeting, and you realize that the only seat left open is the one in the middle of the table facing out to the audience. There you are, knowing that you are going to have to call the meeting to order.

Good, Matt—keep that image. Hold it . . . hold it . . .

Great Matt—let go of the image, focus on your breathing . . . slow, smooth, rhythmic . . .

Okay—good. So, Matt, here you are, walking up on the stage . . . (attempting to represent this scenario).

(Counselor notices that Matt moved his index finger to signify his anxiety is over 5 on his SUDS scale.)

Okay, Matt. . . . take a deep, cleansing breath; relax your body; focus on slow rhythmic relaxing breaths. We'll take a few minutes to relax . . . good . . . slow, rhythmic . . . relaxing breaths . . . good . . . letting go of the tension in your body . . . just nice, slow rhythmic breaths.

(With Matt relaxed, the counselor wants to end the session on a success and thus returns Matt to the item right below this one on the hierarchy.)

Matt, before we stop, for today, I would like you to imagine that you are in Mrs. Federico's class, but you and your "team" just finished your

(Continued)

(Continued)

concluding comments in the affirmative side of the debate. You know you really did well as a group and even your classmates seem in support of your position. Now it's your turn to provide a summary of your group's position. You start to speak and everyone is looking at you ... but you know your group has the best argument ... Then, you hear your voice and it sounds strong and clear.

Now, hold that image and keep your relaxed, smooth breathing ... good ... good ... okay, open your eyes.

Great job today. I want you to keep practicing your relaxation training and maybe we can spend fifteen minutes tomorrow with a couple of other scenarios listed on your hierarchy.

Matt: Sounds great. I'm starting to believe we can do this.

SUMMARY

Counterconditioning

- Counterconditioning is a process by which a response to a particular stimuli is now replaced with a new—incompatible—response.
- This new response, once established, serves to counteract the previous tendency to engage in the identified behavior of concern.
- Counterconditioning employs the fundamental paradigm previously articulated by Ivan Pavlov and identified as respondent conditioning.

Systematic Desensitization

- Desensitization employs counterconditioning to teach the student a new response to the feared stimuli, a response that proves incompatible with, and thus inhibitory of, the previously learned anxiety response.
- Systematic desensitization appears to be a treatment of choice when: (1) anxiety is elicited in the absence of objective danger or threat of real harm, (2) the response pattern of anxiety is causing disruption to adaptive functioning, and (3) maladaptive behaviors have been learned and maintained to alleviate or avoid anxiety.

- Systematic desensitization involves:

  1. Identifying specific stimuli that will be used in the desensitization process.
  2. Helping the student develop an anxiety-inhibiting response, such as deep muscle relaxation.
  3. Presenting those stimuli that will elicit anxiety in such a manner (i.e., hierarchical fashion) that they will never produce an anxiety response at level of intensity greater than the antagonistic response being used. It is this graduated presentation of these anxiety-eliciting stimuli in a sequence of increasing intensity that is the hallmark of systematic desensitization.

Part III

From the Eyes of the Behavioral-Oriented Expert

The previous chapters introduced you the principles, constructs, and strategies of a behavioral-oriented approach to school counseling. However, the primary purpose of this book is to assist counselors in the process of "thinking" like a behaviorally oriented counselor, and not merely understanding principles and concepts. But what does "thinking" like an expert entail?

A review of the literature identifying differences between "expert" and "novice" professionals points to the fact that those with expertise encode, organize, and use client information in ways that facilitate reasoning and problem solving much differently than those new to the profession. Rather than organizing client data into categories that are based on superficial, irrelevant cues that may not be pertinent to generating a solution, experts have organizational cognitive structures, or schemas, which help them quickly make sense of the information that a client presents. Thus, the expert behaviorally oriented school counselor employs that framework to store student data in problem-relevant categories that are connected by underlying conceptual principles relevant to the establishment of a solution. This is the process characterizing the practice of those identified as "experts" (Chi, Feltovich, & Glaser, 1981).

In addition to increasing the counselor's ability to discern the relevant from the irrelevant and to store these data efficiently, experts employ procedural knowledge to guide their interactions in session. The effective counselor, as suggested previously, reflects "on" and "in" session, approaching each encounter by organizing student data into, "If . . . [condition phase], then . . . [action phase]" statements. The expert counselor knows that "if the student presents with this . . . then I'll do that."

Developing the ability to employ a behavioral-orienting framework to guide procedural knowledge of what to do and when to do it is how a school counselor increases his or her effectiveness. Developing procedural knowledge requires that we move beyond simply understanding and storing concepts and constructs and begin to employ these concepts in practice. The final two chapters of this book (Chapters 6 and 7) are designed to support the development of this procedural knowledge using a behavioral-orienting framework to guide you and your reflections "in" and "on" practice.

Chapter 6 provides an in-depth look at two school counselors in action as they address student concerns from a behavioral-orienting framework. Each case provides a look into the methods and strategies employed by a counselor with a behavioral focus. However, more than an illustration of the application of strategies, each case also provides some insight into the counselor's procedural thinking that guides the selection and use of these "strategies." The intent is that by gaining insight into the thinking of the counselors presented, the reader will be able to employ a behavioral orientation to process student data and anticipate the counselors' needed responses. It is in developing that anticipation that you will have employed procedural knowledge from a behavioral orientation, thus "thinking" like the expert!

In Chapter 7, the reader is invited to become an active participant in the processes of reflecting "in" and "on" practice. Student data and verbatim exchange is provided, but Chapter 7 includes, more importantly, a number of at salient points in the encounter that you will be invited to reflect on as the data is presented, and subsequently anticipate the direction to be taken.

School Counselors Reflecting "in" and "on" Practice

6

Chapter 6 provides two case illustrations of school counselors employing a behavioral-orienting framework to guide their reflections "on" and "in" session. It is suggested that you attempt to use your understanding of behavioral principles and techniques to anticipate the illustrative counselors' thinking and subsequent actions. It is in anticipating the counselors' thoughts and actions that you will also employ procedural knowledge from a behavioral-orienting framework and thus "think" like the expert!

In the first case, the counselor illustrates her reflections "on" and "in" practice that guided her decision to include the teacher as a collaborator in both the data collection and treatment planning. The second case illustrates the counselor's ability to engage the student in a process of self-management and the subtle adjustments "in" session that occur as a result of the data reported by the student.

CASE 1: RON

Simply Out of Control!

Starting with the initial intake, the effective school counselor allows his or her counseling decisions to be guided by the processes of reflecting on and in practice. For the counselor operating from a behavioral-orienting framework, a number of markers are set out to guide this reflection and the resulting practice decisions (see Figure 6.1). In this first case, the case of Ron, we will "see" the counselor's reflection as she moves from initial referral to intervention planning.

(Continued)

(Continued)

Figure 6.1   Guiding Reflection "on" and "in" Practice

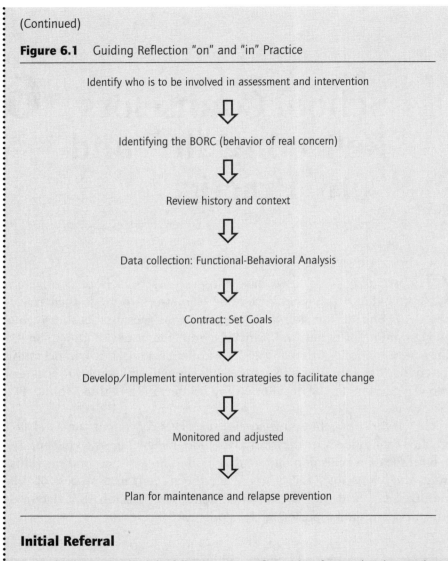

Identify who is to be involved in assessment and intervention

⇩

Identifying the BORC (behavior of real concern)

⇩

Review history and context

⇩

Data collection: Functional-Behavioral Analysis

⇩

Contract: Set Goals

⇩

Develop/Implement intervention strategies to facilitate change

⇩

Monitored and adjusted

⇩

Plan for maintenance and relapse prevention

Initial Referral

Linda Shuster received the following request for services from Judy Johnson, the sixth-grade science teacher. The request read as follows:

Linda, you need to see Ron L ASAP! He is simply out of control.

We are doing "mini-experiments" in class and the students are working in small groups. He does everything he can to be disruptive. He makes obscene sounds—speaks very loud, calling for materials or announcing his observations so that all the students can hear, and once in a while, he'll call out another student's name and say things like "don't touch me you perve!" I've talked with him; I had him come back after school as punishment, and I really don't want to write him up ... but he's out of control. Please help.

—Judy

Reflections "on" Practice

As Ms. Shuster read the referral, she immediately began to "hypothesize" about the function these behaviors may serve. While very mindful of not jumping to conclusions, she was moved to gather some additional information in order to begin hypothesizing about the nature of the BORC, the function it may serve, and the conditions that may be supporting its manifestation. The first question she had was, "Whom should I include in this assessment process?"

While normally she would immediately call a student down to her office, she decided that it might be more productive if she first spoke face-to-face with Ms. Johnson in order to gather additional data. Her concern was that she didn't want to pull Ron from class, if he was having problems, and also she was a little concerned that Ron may actually enjoy leaving class and use his acting out as a means to achieve this end.

Ms. Shuster:	Judy, up for lunch (smiling)?
Ms. Johnson:	Hmm (smiling) . . . a working lunch, I assume?
Ms. S:	I picked up your referral. Wow . . . sounds like Ron is giving you a run for the money?
Ms. J:	You know me . . . I generally handle my own issues in the classroom, but he is driving me crazy and really disrupting the class. I really want you to see him.
Ms. S:	I'll be happy to see him, but I want to get a better feeling over what it is, specifically, that he is doing. I know you said he was disruptive, but could you be a bit more specific as to what it is he does, and when he tends to do it?
Ms. J:	He's generally okay when I'm lecturing or we are doing individual deskwork, but as I said, we have begun doing a lot of mini-experiments, mostly observation and reporting projects, and I have the students working in small groups. It seems as soon as we move to the small groups he starts to act out.
Ms. S:	Act out?

Identifying the BORC

Ms. J:	Well, mostly verbal disruptions. He's been making farting sounds—sorry—and then he calls out usually picking on Rico, saying things like "Rico, stop touching me," or, "Rico, don't be so weird."
Ms. S:	So, it seems like this disruption generally happens during the lab work and is generally verbal in form. Does it take any other form? Like does he break or bang things, or walk around or touch other students?

(Continued)

(Continued)

Ms. J: No, it really is just verbal. But he's loud, and when he engages other students like Rico, I'm afraid this is going to escalate.

Ms. S: So, what we are calling disruptive is Ron calling out, making noises, and calling out other students' names. Is that pretty much what we are looking at? (defining the BORC)

Ms. J: Yep . . .

History and Context

Ms. S: It's interesting that he doesn't do this while at his desk doing deskwork, or when you are teaching a lesson. Has he done this before?

Ms. J: No, that's the thing that caught me off guard. He's been a really good student—really active and involved. But it seems that this lab time is his clue to play!

Reflection "in" Practice (Ms. Shuster)

Judy is clearly frustrated and with all that she is doing in class, I don't want to ask her to gather any more data—but I do want her involved in the interpretation and intervention planning.

Identifying Who Is Involved
in Assessment and Intervention

Ms. S: I wonder if it would be valuable for me to come and try to watch what is going on in and around the time he acts this way. Maybe if I could observe him doing it, along with the events that seem to be associated with his behavior, we might have a better sense of what's going on.

Ms. J: I'd love it!

Ms. S: Now, he may act a little different if he sees me in the room, so I may need to come in a couple of times just to "hang out." Would that be okay?

Ms. J: Absolutely.

Ms. S: Super. Can we "do lunch" on Friday (smiling)? We can talk more about what went on and maybe together come up with some ideas about what to do?

Reflection "on" Practice (following lunch with Judy)

I'm not sure what's going on, but I wonder if:

1. Ron is going out of his way to gain some attention—but if so, whose?

2. Or, I wonder if he is using this disruptive behavior to escape or avoid engaging in the assigned work.

3. Either way, I have to figure out how to be unobtrusive in class so I can gather notes on the conditions surrounding this behavior.

Data Collection: Functional-Behavioral Analysis (FBA)

Reflection "on" Practice (prior to observing class)

Judy said that she tends to walk around the class, and she takes notes that she discusses with the class. I am assuming they are "desensitized" to her note taking, so I think I'll keep a narrative report of what I'm observing.

Ms. J: Class, we have a guest today, Ms. Shuster.

Ms. S: Hi, all (greeting students). I'm going to join you today and see if I can learn anything from you—"mad scientists" (smiling).

Ms. J: Okay. So, we all know what we are doing and you have your assignments, so let's get started. Remember, pay close attention and provide very detailed descriptions about what you observe.

(Class begins working, and Ms. Johnson walks about as Ms. Shuster follows along, writing structured anecdotal notes.)

Data Analysis: FBA

(Two days later, Ms. Shuster shares observations with Ms. Johnson.)

Ms. S: Hi, Judy . . . great class. The kids were really into it.

Ms. J: Thanks, yeah . . . into it . . . especially our pal.

Ms. S: It was kind of amazing that he seemed to start as soon as he got to the table.

Ms. J: Yep . . . that's what I was telling you.

(Continued)

(Continued)

Ms. S: Well, I gathered some observations...but let me set the stage a little. Before I went in, I had a couple of "working hypotheses" about what was going on...

Ms. J: Oh, look at you (smiling)—"hypotheses"—little miss scientist.

Reflections "in" Practice

Judy is really a joy to work with. And, I love her scientist orientation. I think she'll be open to "experiment" with interventions and let the data guide us.

Ms. S: Sometimes it helps (smiling). So, anyway, I was wondering if he was acting out to gain somebody's or maybe anybody's attention, or if he was doing this as a way of avoiding doing the lab work?

Ms. J: He's really bright and has an inquisitive scientific mind, so I doubt he's avoiding the experiments.

Ms. S: Right on! The data I collected doesn't seem to suggest he's avoiding the work, since even when he's making noises he's actively observing and writing his observations down. So, how about the alternative hypothesis?

Ms. J: Attention getting?

Ms. S: Yep...

Ms. J: But whose...I am really careful about not reinforcing that behavior.

Reflection "on" Practice

Judy was actually very careful at attending to Ron only when he was on task, but he was certainly testing her. She seems to understand the principles of reinforcement and extinction.

Ms. S: Oh, look at you (smiling)...Ms. behavioral scientist...reinforcing! I'm only kidding. You are right on. You have him working in the same group as Lauren and it appears that he enjoys her giggles. Look here (pointing to data). I started to record each time he called out or made a noise, and then I watched what happened right afterwards. Every time he did that...he looked at Lauren and she was giggling!

Ms. J: Oh, great, hormones and adolescents.

Ms. S: Well, I'm not sure it's that simple, but I'm sure that is involved.

Ms. J: I guess I should move them to different groups?

Ms. S: The only concern I have there is that since his noise making has been working, he may just get louder so that she still hears him and reacts. If that happens, it may be even more disruptive.

Ms. J: Well, okay, now what?

Contract: Setting Goals

Ms. S: Well, I know you wanted me to see Ron but I'm wondering if you would be interested in trying a little experiment. Maybe seeing if we can reduce his disruptive behavior right in class?

Ms. J: I've tried lots of things, but nothing is working.

Ms. S: Well, you certainly tried all the things I would have used to redirect him and correct him. But now that we think he's working hard to get Lauren's "giggles," I wonder if we could come up with some strategies to try. You know, like a mini-experiment—try something and collect data on his behavior and see where we go. I could always call him down, but this may be easier and faster?

Ms. J: Sounds interesting, but I'm not sure what we can do.

Reflections "in" Practice

Judy is very curious and ready to go. But, she has a lot on her plate, so whatever we try can't be too cumbersome or difficult, or she may not be able to be consistent in the application.

Developing/Implementing Intervention Strategies

Ms. S: Well, could we spend some time after school today and go over my observations?

Ms. J: Sure.

Reflections "on" Practice

It seems really clear from these data that when Ron is standing next to Lauren at the lab table, he exhibits the various verbal disruptions and each time it is followed by her giggling. It appears her response is reinforcing his behavior. I wonder how we can extinguish his behavior. I wonder if we could get Lauren to stop giggling at his disruptions.

(Continued)

(Continued)

Ms. S: As I was waiting to meet with you, I was looking over my notes, and it really seems that he is acting out to get Lauren's attention.

Ms. J: Should I talk with her?

Ms. S: Well, we could try that, but I wonder if that would make her uncomfortable or even be fair to Ron?

Ms. J: Oh, yeah. I guess I could separate them?

Ms. S: That would certainly make it harder for her to hear his commentary, but I'm wondering if he may just get louder. Or, if he would perform for whomever his partner may be? You know, when I was watching them work on the observations I saw you had Lauren describing the observations, and Ron was recording the findings in their logs.

Ms. J: Yeah, it just happened that way, with no real rhyme or reason.

Ms. S: It seemed that it was during the brief periods that Lauren was adjusting the solutions—that during those lulls in her descriptions—that's when he started his verbal comments. So, I am wondering what the possible effect would be if we changed the arrangement?

Ms. J: You mean, have Ron do the observing and reporting and have Lauren journal the notes? I like that idea. Maybe that would keep him focused on the task and not Lauren.

Ms. S: It may also allow him to get Lauren's attention for doing something that is desirable—you know, doing the task, rather than being off task.

Ms. J: I like it and I certainly can rearrange things. But I'll probably do it for the whole class rather than just their pairing.

Ms. S: That's a great idea. Now, also, I'm wondering if we can reduce the opportunity or even the need for his disruptive verbalizing by rearranging the roles? I wonder if it would help for you to be especially attentive and kind of "catch him, or catch them at being good!"

Ms. J: Not sure what you mean?

Ms. S: Well. Let's assume that he starts describing the observation and she's recording . . . maybe you could find a way to praise them for working as a team.

Ms. J: Oh, sure . . . I do that stuff all the time with the other groups; it's just that, sadly, his behavior has made me feel like I want to avoid him. And actually, as I said, he's a good student and seems to like the attention for interacting with me during the lecture, so I bet that may work.

Ms. S: Well, at least as we are envisioning it, it seems like a possibility, but how about if we, actually you, give it a try and maybe we could "do lunch" (smiling) on Friday and discuss it?

Ms. J: Definitely can do that, especially if lunch is on you (smiling). Do you think it may be useful if you stop in today or tomorrow and do your observation thing? Sometimes I get so busy that I may not really be able to pick up how it's going.

Ms. S: Great idea. I could come in today and tomorrow for a little while and simply hang out and observe like I did before. We could analyze those data to see how we are doing.

Ms. J: I'm going to make a scientist out of you (laughing)...yet!

Although we leave this case at this point in its development, monitoring the impact of this "intervention" and making any needed modification (including talking to Lauren, or Lauren and Ron) would be the next part of the process, as would planning for termination and relapse prevention.

CASE 2: ROSIE

A Process of Self-Monitoring

Rosie is a six-year-old Latina who has been diagnosed with ADHD. Rosie's first-grade teacher, Ms. Burwell, sought assistance from the school counselor, Tim Hansen, in helping Rosie stay on task. Specifically, the teacher noted that Rosie displayed off-task behaviors that included playing with her pencils or other supplies, removing herself from her seat at inappropriate times, and physically touching her peers. Ms. Burwell attempted to correct these behaviors with verbal reprimands and time-outs, but these have not proven successful.

Reflection "on" Practice (Mr. Hansen)

I'm not familiar with Rosie and I'm really not clear about when these off-task behaviors occur. I want to meet with Ms. Burwell to see if we can get a better sense of what is going on and when it occurs.

Identifying the BORC: History and Context

Ms. Burwell: Hi, Tim. How's it going?

Mr. Hansen: Hi, Maryellen. Really well, thanks. It sounds like you have your hands full with Rosie?

(Continued)

(Continued)

Ms. B: Good kid . . . but boy is she tough to manage.

Mr. H: I got the sense that she has some difficulty staying on task. Could you give me some of the details?

Ms. B: Well, it really only happens during reading instruction. She's in, or beginning, reading sequence and the curriculum is pretty systematized. It focuses on sequenced, repetitive sight-word learning. So, I work with the kids in small groups and we start with prereading activities, then word recognition, and then direction cards and picture/phrase cards, storybooks, and test. Well, she is okay as long as I'm directing the activity, but as soon as she has to work on her picture/phrase cards or any seat directed activity, she's good for about thirty seconds and then wow, watch out.

Mr. H: Okay, so it generally happens during the reading instruction. I'm not sure what you mean by "wow, watch out"?

Ms. B: That's a little dramatic . . . I just meant . . . she gets off task very rapidly.

Mr. H: Off task—what would that look like?

Ms. B: Well, I guess any time she starts using the materials inappropriately, like playing with the cards or throwing the book up in the air.

Mr. H: Okay, good. Anything else that would indicate she's off task?

Ms. B: Well, she gets out of her seat without permission and she will start talking with another student. She has even started poking the students beside her.

Mr. H: Got it. So, would on-task behavior include reading the words, responding to your questions, speaking when recognized and spoken to?

Ms. B: Yep.

Reflection "in" Practice

I think I have a clear picture of the BORC but I wonder how often it really occurs and what the context is in which it occurs?

Data Collection: Functional-Behavioral Analysis (FBA)

Mr. H: Maryellen, would it be possible for me to come and observe Rosie? I would like to get a better feel for how often this occurs, and if there is anything going on that may stimulate it or keep it going?

Ms. B: Sure . . . but it feels like it goes on the entire time.

Mr. H: I bet it does feel that way.

Reflection "in" Practice

Ms. Burwell sounds a bit frustrated. I want to be sure that I affirm her work to this point and set a stage for positive expectations.

Mr. H: You know the things you tried—the time-out and soft reprimands— would be strategies I would have considered, so I am really curious to see what else may be going on. You have given me a super description of the "off-task" behavior. So, if you are up for it, I'll come and see if I can catch anything and then you and I can do some brainstorming on what to try next.

Ms. B: I'm open for suggestions (smiling).

Reflection "on" Practice

I think I'll try to measure off-task behavior using a stopwatch. When Rosie begins engaging in the off-task behaviors, I'll start timing and stop as soon as she re-engages in on-task behavior. I probably should observe at least for two days, during the thirty-minute reading period.

Mr. H: Hi, Maryellen—wow—I have to tell you, I'm impressed.

Ms. B: Yeah, right.

Mr. H: No, seriously. Your classroom is so alive and cheery and really all the students seem to love you . . . even Rosie!

Ms. B: Ah, she's a good kid . . . just tough to manage.

Mr. H: Well, you can say that again. In observing her for the past two days, I recorded the total time she was off task and look here (pointing to data sheet), Wednesday she had total of sixteen minutes, out of the thirty-minute instructional period, off task and then Thursday, thirteen minutes off task, so I can certainly see why you're concerned.

Ms. B: Yikes . . . I didn't realize it was almost half the period.

Mr. H: Yeah, and I couldn't find anything specific that would trigger the behavior or anything that she was attempting to get—you know, like your attention or something?

(Continued)

(Continued)

Ms. B: I know. That's what makes it really hard.

Mr. H: I'm not even sure that Rosie is aware that she's off task?

Ms. B: That's funny, because when I would reprimand her, she would become very apologetic and say she didn't know why she was poking, or out of her seat, poor kid.

Mr. H: Well, that gives me an idea. I wonder if you think it would be okay if I met with Rosie and maybe she and I could discuss some things that we could try to help?

Ms. B: Give it a shot.

Mr. H: Not so fast (smiling)...I know once I meet with her, I am going to get you involved.

Ms. B: This close to an escape (smiling).

Reflection "on" Practice

I remember reading somewhere, wish I could remember where...about teaching students to self-monitor their on-task behavior. I should find that study.

Developing/Implementing Intervention Strategies

Reflection "on" Practice

I am going to try this process, one I found in an article on self-monitoring, with Rosie.

Mr. H: Hi Rosie, come on in—really nice to see you.

Rosie: (Enters, smiling, and looks about the room.)

Mr. H: Rosie, would you come over here (pointing to the chair) and have a seat? I want to talk with you.

Rosie: What about (sitting)? You know I've been to a counselor before?

Mr. H: You have?

Rosie: Yeah, my mom and dad took me a couple of times and we played games.

Mr. H: That sounds really neat...Well, maybe you and I could play a little game after we talk for a moment.

Rosie:	I know Ms. Burwell wanted me to talk with you, 'cause I'm not doing so good.
Mr. H:	Well, you are right that Ms. Burwell wanted me to talk with you, but not because you are doing poorly, but because she wanted me to help you figure out a way you could stay in your seat and really do your work during reading time.
Rosie:	I do.
Mr. H:	You know what? You are right. When I was in yesterday . . .
Rosie:	(Interrupts) . . . Yeah, I saw you and you had a stopwatch, my dad has one of those . . .
Mr. H:	Yep, I had a stopwatch, and what I found out was that during reading time, you are really able to do your work for a big part of the time, but then you also spent time doing other things like playing with the picture cards or getting out of your seat.
Rosie:	I know (getting upset), Ms. Burwell use to holler at me . . .
Mr. H:	Well, no one is angry, but we have an idea that maybe will help you stay in your seat, like the other kids, and really do your best during reading. Okay?
Rosie:	Okay.
Mr. H:	Now, don't be so worried. I bet this will be fun. See this piece of paper? (Looks at a self-monitoring paper that has ten lines, each with a smiling face and a frowning face.) I am going to ask you to try something. I am going to ask Ms. Burwell if I could put this tape recorder under your desk, you know, where you have your books. And, during reading time, I am going to ask her to turn it on. Now listen (turning on the tape). Nothing is happening but wait. (A little bell rings.) Did you hear that?
Rosie:	Yeah . . . that's cute.
Mr. H	Yep. During your reading time, that bell will ring once in a while, and when it does, I want you to circle one of these faces.
Rosie:	I like the smiley face.
Mr. H:	Me too . . . but you can only circle the smiley *if* you are in your seat and you are doing your reading work. Okay?
Rosie:	Okay.
Mr. H:	And, when the bell goes off . . . if you are looking around the room or out of your seat or playing with your materials and *not* doing your reading, then you should circle the frowning face. Okay?

(Continued)

(Continued)

Rosie: Yeah . . . I'm going to be doing my work and get smiley faces.

Mr. H: That's super!

Mr. H: Let's try it out . . . like pretend. This will be our game. Today, Ms. Burwell gave me the cards you used yesterday, and told me that you took the cards and made them into a story by arranging them in order. Is that what you did?

Rosie: Yeah, it was fun.

Mr. H: Okay. So, I would like you to do that again, and this time, we'll turn on the tape recorder and every time you hear a bell, circle either a smiley face if you are working hard, or a frowning face if you are not doing the reading task. Okay?

Rosie: Yep (smiling).

Reflection "in" Practice

Rosie is really a bright little girl and is really into this. I was concerned that she would be distracted by the bell, but she's doing a great job.

Mr. H: Rosie, that was super! And look, the bell rang five times, and each time, you were working on your story . . . fantastic! Five smiley faces.

Rosie: Told you!

Mr. H: Yes, you did. Now I'll tell Ms. Burwell what we are doing, and tomorrow she'll give you the smiley sheet and turn on the bells . . . but your job is to work at your reading and circle a face each time the bell rings. Okay?

Rosie: They are all going to be smiley faces.

Mr. H: Well, do your best and I'll see you tomorrow.

Reflection "on" Practice

I'll meet with Ms. Burwell today and explain what we are doing and how it went. I want to see Rosie for a couple of days—at least until the end of the week to be sure she is following the procedure but I also want Ms. Burwell to be very active in praising her for her successes.

Monitoring

Ms. B: Tim, Rosie's behavior has really improved. The smiley-face thing is really cool. Look here, even when she places a frowning face, it is because she's looking around. She hasn't gotten out of her seat or physically touched another student in the past ten days.

Mr. H: That's super . . . and she's really proud. Even though I'm not seeing her each day, she finds a way to stop in on her way home to tell me she's a "smiley face" girl . . . that's her term.

Ms. B: She's been super. I am wondering if we could start to wean the tape recorder?

Reflection "in" Practice

That's funny. Ms. Burwell is a step ahead of me. The idea of fading the tape recorder and moving toward a more natural form of monitoring was on my things-to-do list.

Mr. H: Absolutely. Is the tape a problem for the other students?

Ms. B: No, I just thought it might be time.

Mr. H: Well, we could do it a couple of different ways. We could just stop the tape and have you circle a smiley face or frowning face; or we lengthen the period of time between bells . . .

Ms. B: You know, I would like to try just leaving the recording sheet on her desk and I will go over and "catch her" at being good and circle the smiley faces . . . and then maybe use the frowning face to signal when she's really off task?

Mr. H: I like the idea. I guess the best thing to do is give it a shot and we can see how she does. I really do think she's more aware, and with your praise and attention, she'll continue to strengthen her on-task behaviors.

Follow-Up

Ms. Burwell was able to fade out not just the recorder, but even the smiley-face chart. Rosie was more easily directed to task at those times when she was off task by Ms. Burwell simply making a "frown" or a "smile." Rosie was able to use those teacher's nonverbal prompts to get back to task.

FINAL THOUGHTS

In the final chapter, Chapter 7, you will once again be provided case illustrations. However, this time, in addition to observing a school counselor operating with behavioral orientation as the frame of reference, you will be invited to participate. At various points in the case presentation, you will be asked to reflect on what is happening and what it is that you would do next in the process. The hope is that by stepping into the dialogue, you will be able to translate your understanding of the behavioral model into its application.

Practice in Procedural Thinking

7

T he previous chapter presented examples of counselors employing a behavioral orientation as they reflected "on" and "in" their practice. The cases illustrated the counselors' procedural thinking as they responded to the material and information provided by the students and/or teachers with whom they were working. The current chapter invites you to move beyond simply observing the procedural thinking of a counselor with a behavioral orientation, to actually engaging in that very process.

This final chapter provides the case of Randall. It is a case that illustrates a process of moving from the initial "hello" through termination. As you read the case material, you will note places where the counselor is reflecting "in" or "on" practice and using that reflection to guide her actions. However, prior to viewing the counselor's reflection and decision, you will be invited to use a behavioral-oriented framework or lens to process the data presented and anticipate the counselor's response. It is hoped that with this type of practice, you will move from understanding the concepts and constructs of behavioral theory to employing a behavioral framework to guide your own reflections "on" and "in" practice.

One final note is important to understand prior to reviewing the case. This case of Randall, the sixth-grade bully, is employed in the companion texts within this series. The reason for this replication is that it will provide readers the opportunity to compare and contrast the variations in reflections and practice of school counselors operating with varied orienting frameworks.

RANDALL: THE SIXTH-GRADE BULLY

History and Context

Tammy Schulman is the middle-school counselor at E. L. Richardson Middle School. Ms. Schulman receives a referral from the assistant principal that reads:

> *Tammy, I've been hearing numerous complaints from teachers and students alike about Randall Jenkins. While we are only three weeks into the school year, Randall has already accrued ten demerits for fighting. It is clear that unless we do something, Randall won't be here by midterm. Please see him as soon possible.*

Reflection "on" Practice

Assuming you are a school counselor with a behavioral orientation, what would you do upon receiving this referral?

Ms. Schulman does not know Randall, so she wants to see if there are any data that would suggest possible explanations for this behavior and strategies that may have been used by his previous counselors. As such, she reviews his cumulative folder. Ms. Schulman discovers very little information in the folder. Randall is a recent transfer to E. L. Richardson and his previous school has yet to send relevant files. However, what Ms. Schulman does discover is that Randall is new to the district, after moving here with his mother following his parents' divorce. As Ms. Schulman sits waiting for Randall to come down in response to her request to see him, she reflects on what she hopes to accomplish as a result of this initial meeting.

Reflection "on" Practice

If you were the school counselor in this situation and operating from a behavioral frame of reference, what goals might you have for this initial session and how might you go about achieving these?

As she sits at her desk, Ms. Schulman jots down a couple of reminders: "collaboration," "empathy," "clarity" and "concreteness." It is clear from her notes that she anticipates that Randall may enter counseling unsure of the need or value of the counseling and may in fact be defensive and in need of support. While hoping to identify Randall's goals, Ms. Schulman clearly values the need to build a working alliance with Randall and, if possible, to begin to identify and concretely define the behavior of real concern (BORC).

First Session

Ms. Schulman:	Randall, come in. Thanks for coming. I'm Ms. Schulman, the sixth-grade counselor.
Randall:	(Looks down, and sits without talking.)
Ms. S:	Randall, do you know why I asked to see you?
Randall:	(Still looks down, and shows little response.)
Ms. S:	Randall, you look a little uncomfortable, are you mad at me for some reason?
Randall:	(Looks up, somewhat surprised by the question.)
Ms. S:	Thanks for looking up. I wasn't sure if I was doing something wrong, because you look really unhappy. Are you unhappy right now?
Randall:	(Nods yes, still not talking.)

Reflection "in" Practice

As the counselor working from a behavioral orientation, how do you interpret and respond to Randall's initial presentation?

Looking at Randall, Ms. Schulman "feels" as if he is building a self-protected buttress—arms crossed, chin on his chest, looking down, and showing minimal responses. Her read is that he is preparing for an assault and clearly being defensive. It appears that Randall has learned to associate meetings with the counselor or one-on-ones with an adult in school as a cue for a negative encounter. With this interpretation, she feels that she needs to demonstrate support and encouragement and invite Randall to set the direction for the session.

Ms. S:	Randall, I am really sorry that you are unhappy. I wish I could help, but I am really amazed that even being this unhappy, you were still able to come down here and meet with me.
Randall:	I had to come—you sent for me.
Ms. S:	Yes, I guess that is correct, but you did come and I appreciate that, and really appreciate you talking with me now.
Randall:	Yeah, okay.

Reflection "in" Practice

Randall has opened a tiny bit. At this point sensing his immediate problem of being "unhappy" and apparently defensive, what might your next move be?

(Continued)

(Continued)

   With Randall at least now showing some minimal willingness to engage verbally, Ms. Schulman wonders if it would help to share with Randall what she had been told and what her goals may be.

Ms. S: Randall, you are correct in that I did want to meet with you. I was talking to Dr. Kim and he was telling me that you have had a little problem with some of the other kids in school. I was hoping you would tell me a little about what has been going on?

Randall: It's not my fault (looking down).

Ms. S: It's not your fault? Okay . . . but what is the "it"?

Randall: Fighting.

Ms. S.   Randall, you know what? It would really help me if you could tell me about the fighting.

Randall: Like what?

Ms. S: Well, how many times have you gotten in trouble for fighting here at school?

Randall: I was sent to Dr. Kim once because Boston and I were pushing each other in lunch line and then I went to Dr. Kim because Chuck Hammel and I got into an argument in the bathroom and then started pushing each other, until Mr. Allison stopped it.

Ms. S: Oh, so it was two times and both times "fighting" really was a matter of pushing another student?

Randall: Yeah, but Dr. Kim is really mad and on my case about it.

Ms. S: That sounds like you would like it better if Dr. Kim wasn't on your case.

Randall: Yeah, everybody is trying to get me in trouble.

Ms. S: Wow. You know, it would help me if you could tell me a little more about one of these incidents and how it came about.

Randall: What do you mean?

Ms. S: Well, maybe you could describe what you were doing before it started, then what happened immediately before you got into the pushing, and even what happened afterwards.

Reflection "in" Practice

While we are not sure if Randall will be able to accurately report on these incidents, what do you think Ms. Schulman may be looking for?

Ms. Schulman is beginning to wonder if the pushing was elicited by some antecedent condition or if it is a behavior that effectively helps Randall achieve some desired consequence.

Randall:	Well, Boston just cut in front of me in lunch line and he said real loud so everybody could hear it, "What are you lookin' at loser?" Then the other kids in line started making noises like "oooh" "get him" and that kind of stuff.
Ms. S:	Boston? I assume you mean Ralph? So, Boston just cut in front of you and called you a name and then the other kids started to encourage you to do something?
Randall:	Yeah . . . and then Boston, I mean Ralph, just kept lookin' at me and then said something like you want to do something about it—homo. . and then I pushed him.
Ms. S:	Randall, thanks for sharing that. What happened after you pushed him?
Randall:	Ah . . . he pushed back but then Mrs. Jacobs pulled us out of line and told us to go see Dr. Kim.
Ms. S:	Anything else happen before you left the cafeteria? Like, did the other kids do anything?
Randall:	I don't think so . . . we just went to the office.
Ms. S:	Oh, okay. How did that compare to the situation in the bathroom?
Randall:	It was after gym and I went to the bathroom and a couple of other guys from gym were in there, and Chuck said real loud as I walked in . . . "hey homo" and then everybody started to laugh.
Ms. S:	So the other guys started to laugh? What happened next?
Randall:	I was going to the stall and Chuck was going to the sink and he gave me a shove.
Ms. S:	So he pushed you first?
Randall:	Well, he kind of bumped me as we passed, but then he called me a name and the other guys started to yell "get him" and I just pushed him into the sink.
Ms. S:	Oh, so he called you a name and then other guys started encouraging you and you pushed him?
Randall:	Yeah, and that's when Mr. Allison came in and told me to go to Dr. Kim's office.

(Continued)

(Continued)

Ms. S: Randall, I'm wondering. It seems that in both situations the fact that somebody was calling you a name and the other students were saying things like "get him"...that those things kind of led to the pushing?

Randall: I guess (looking down). I kind of have a short fuse.

Reflection "in" Practice

It seems that Ms. Schulman is starting to develop a hypothesis about the nature of Randall's BORC. What are your feelings about the BORC and what may be the choice of intervention?

Ms. Schulman is hypothesizing that Randall's behavior is more reactive than proactive. It doesn't seem he is trying to use this "pushing" to gain something, like reactions from the other students or some position of power, but rather, it is his response to being challenged. If that is true, she wonders if some alternative response training may be useful.

Ms. S: So, you have a short fuse? Did you get in a lot of trouble at your old school for fighting?

Randall: No, not really—but then I knew most of the guys. We all went through elementary school together. But I did get ejected from a couple of basketball games because of some fighting.

Ms. S: Basketball games?

Randall: Yeah. Last year, our community-center team was in the championship and the guy who was playing me started saying things...I told him to shut up...and he just kept it up and then he said something about my mom so I pushed him. The ref saw it and ejected me.

Ms. S: Wow. I bet that was disappointing?

Randall: Yeah, we won, but I couldn't play the whole last quarter.

Ms. S: It sounds like sometimes this short fuse really costs you?

Randall: What?

Ms. S: Well, here's a case where a player was able to get you ejected just by calling you names, and the guys here know how to get you sent to Dr. Kim. All they have to do is call you names or give you attitude. I know you didn't like seeing Dr. Kim and definitely didn't like getting ejected. So, that's what I meant by your short fuse costing you.

Randall: Yeah, but I've always had a temper.

Ms. S: You know what? If you are interested, maybe you and I could work on that short fuse? If nothing else, (smiling) maybe we can help you from getting ejected from any other games?

Randall: Yeah (smiling) . . . they need me.

Ms. S: Super. So what do you say if you and I get together a couple times and see if we can work out a plan to deal with name-calling and getting attitude in a way that won't get you ejected?

Reflection "in" Practice

Randall appears to have a reason to work with Ms. Schulman and she has an initial hypothesis about what is going on. She is coming to the end of this session, so what do you feel she may suggest as a homework?

Ms. Schulman is thinking it may be useful if she could gather a few more incidents that she could use to test her hypothesis about the stimulus-response connection, and maybe even use them to demonstrate that connection of name-calling and pushing to Randall.

Ms. S: Randall, you've been a big help by describing a couple of situations that pushed your button. It would be really helpful if you could maybe jot down a couple of other times—like in basketball or maybe at your old school—when somebody pushed your button by calling you a name or giving you attitude. We could look at that and then figure out how to "remove" that button . . .

Randall: Yeah, that would be cool. I could do that. When should I show you?

Ms. S: Well, how about you come see me tomorrow at lunchtime? We could eat together and see if we can figure out a way to be sure you will never get ejected again!

Randall: Okay.

Ms. S: Great, so I'll see you tomorrow and, in the meantime, get back in the "game," but now, just try your best not to hear any of the name-calling—no need to get ejected again!

Randall: No way (smiling).

(Continued)

(Continued)

Reflection "on" Practice

Randall has become engaged and is clearly cooperating with the counselor. What do you anticipate the data may show?

Ms. Schulman, reflecting on the interaction, is encouraged by Randall's engagement in the dialogue and feels like he is beginning to own the problem of his "short fuse" and is also clearly open to finding a solution. She is assuming the data will show that his behavior is respondent to specific cues, like name-calling, and that if this is the case, maybe she can help him develop an alternative response to these stimuli.

Second Session

Ms. S: So, Randall, how did you do?

Randall: Still in the game (smiling).

Ms. S: That's great. How about the note taking? Were you able to remember any other times somebody pushed your button?

Randall: Yeah, I had a couple . . . not many. I think three.

Ms. S: Great. Look, let me make a little chart and then you can start to tell me about these situations. I already started it with the three situations you told me about yesterday. See . . . (pointing to the chart).

Figure 7.1   Randall's A-B-C Log

Antecedent	Behavior	Consequence
Playing in basketball game: player is calling him names and "cuts" up on his mom.	Pushes the player.	Ejected.
Standing in lunch line: student cuts in and calls him a name. Other students encourage a reaction.	Pushes the student.	Sent to Dr. Kim for demerits.
Entering boys' bathroom: he encounters other classmates. One calls him a name and bumps him.	Pushes the student into the sink.	Sent to Dr. Kim for demerits.

Ms. S: See, I broke it down into what was happening right before you pushed and then what happened right after you pushed. I think if we look at these things, we may be able to figure out what we can do.

	Why don't you tell me what you wrote and I'll take notes and place them on this chart.

Randall: Okay. Well, one time, we were having field day, like class day, and this really weird kid kept throwing water balloons at me. I told him I didn't want to do that, I wanted to shoot baskets, but he kept following me and bugging me and calling me a girly-girl and just kept on me, so I turned around and pushed him and teacher saw me and sent me to the principal.

Ms. S: Okay . . . what happened then?

Randall: Nothing, except I was not able to participate in any of the fifth-grade class day activities.

Ms. S: That was a shame . . . I wrote it down. Do you have another?

Randall: Yeah, this just happened the other day. I was playing basketball with my older brother, Jamal, and he charged into me. I went down on the driveway and scraped my elbow. It hurt and I guess I started to tear up a little, but it really hurt. And he's a jerk and he started calling me a crybaby and a little girl . . . things like that. Well, I pushed him and he punched me and then my dad grounded both of us.

Ms. S: Sorry to hear about that, but it's helpful. I think you said you had one more (taking notes).

Randall: Yeah, not a real big deal. In my old school, we had this crazy kid, he got kicked out . . . anyway, we were in class and he sat behind me and he kept flicking my hair with his pen. I used to have long hair. I told him to stop but he kept it up and oh, yeah, he was calling me a long hair freak and girly and stuff like that . . . anyway, I turned and grabbed his shirt collar and told him to stop it. The teacher just saw me and sent me to the principal.

Reflection "in" Practice

Randall has really done some great work. How would you respond to Randall? In reviewing his descriptions and the data presented in the A-B-C logs, what do you feel is the best approach to intervention?

Ms. Schulman, reflecting on the data provided, is really impressed by how conscientious Randall was about the assignment. She wants to reinforce him and also begin to "teach" him about the stimulus-response connection.

(Continued)

(Continued)

Ms. S: Wow, I am really impressed by the work you did and you know what? You actually seem to have a pretty good fuse. I mean, you didn't freak out immediately in any of these situations . . . but I can see how if they keep pushing you, then it seems like it is hard for you not to respond?

Randall: It's like a switch goes off and I just push them.

Ms. S: Randall, if we look all of these situations (pointing to the logs), I notice something right away.

Figure 7.2 Randall's A-B-C Log: Added Situations

Antecedent	Behavior	Consequence
During fifth-grade class day, another student kept throwing water balloons at me and when I told him to stop he started calling me a bunch of names and kept following me around the school yard just saying the names over and over and I told him to stop but he didn't . . . so I turned and pushed him.	I pushed him down on the ground.	I was sent to principal and not allowed to participate in class-day activities.
I was playing some basketball with my brother Jamal and he charged me and knocked me down. It hurt and I started to cry and he started teasing me calling me a baby, a little girl.	I pushed him in the chest.	He punched me and my dad grounded both of us for the weekend.
I was in class one time and the kid behind kept flicking my hair with his pen . . . my hair was long and he kept calling me "girly-girl" and other things. I told him to shut up. He kept it up.	I grabbed his collar and told him to stop it.	The teacher sent me to the principal's office.

Randall: What (looking at the logs)?

Ms. S: Let me explain something. Sometimes people push other people or get into fights because it helps them get something they want . . .

Randall: You mean like if I beat you up to get your money?

Ms. S: Exactly!

Randall: Or to impress my friends . . .

Ms. S:	Wow, right on! But look here (pointing to consequences). None of the things you got following your pushing seemed like something you wanted.
Randall:	No way—especially the grounding and the ejection from the game. I hated that.
Ms. S:	So, if we assume that you are not doing these things because you like what it gets you, then we go over here (pointing to the antecedent column) and see if there is something here that works like a "trigger" to create your reaction.
Randall:	A trigger?
Ms. S:	Well, like something that pushes your button.
Randall:	Okay.
Ms. S:	So, if we look down this column, it seems like "name-calling" is something that acts to push your button and it seems to result in you pushing the other person.
Randall:	Well, if they'd stop picking on me then I wouldn't push.

Reflection "in" Practice

Randall is certainly following along, but like many people, he seems to place the issue of control to outside circumstances. What might you do at this juncture to "empower" him?

Ms. Schulman certainly can't disagree with Randall, but she wants him to be motivated to take control over this situation, rather than hope and rely on the goodness of others. She also wants to find a way to increase his motivation to do the work that will need to be done.

Ms. S:	You are absolutely correct. But, let me tell you a little secret. If I was the coach of an opposing basketball team, and I knew that we could get your team's best player, that's you (smiling), ejected by calling you some names…what do you think? Do you think I would stop?
Randall:	No way (smiling).
Ms. S:	So, maybe rather than you and me hoping they'll stop, maybe we should figure out how to develop a different response to those

(Continued)

(Continued)

triggers. Just think about it... if every time the opposing player was busy calling you names, rather than you telling him to shut up or pushing him, you just dribbled past him and made a shot. Do you think he would eventually stop the name-calling?

Randall: Yeah... cool!

Ms. S: So, we have to figure out, what would be a better way for you to respond to these name-callers?

Reflection "in" Practice

So, the target for the intervention appears to be developing an alternative response to name-calling. In what ways might you consider the use of modeling, shaping, and reinforcement in your development of an intervention strategy?

As Ms. Schulman reflects in session, she decides to see if a hierarchy of situations could be developed ranging from those in which Randall employed alternative responses to name-calling through those that really seemed to be a strong trigger for eliciting his pushing behavior.

Ms. S: Randall, you have described a couple of situations where the trigger was really strong and you reacted by pushing. I'm wondering, have there ever been times when someone has called you a name and you used some other way to respond?

Randall: You mean like if my brother is saying something and I tell him to shut up?

Ms. S: I guess. But I'm wondering if there are times when someone calls you a name, and you just ignore it... you know, walk away or just keep doing what you are doing?

Randall: I don't know... I guess.

Ms. S: Well, we have a few minutes. Maybe we could try something.

Reflection "in" Practice

What would you be "trying" in the remaining minutes of the session... something that may help you with the shaping process?

Ms. Schulman wants to begin to identify some subgoals that can be used in shaping. She hopes to establish a hierarchy where the strength of the triggers will go from very little to intense.

Ms. S: I am not a very good artist, but let me try something. This is a magnet (drawing a horseshoe-shaped magnet on the paper) and over here (drawing a stick figure) is you . . .

Randall: Yikes . . . pretty skinny (smiling). You know, I like to draw.

Ms. S: You do, fantastic. Let me show you what I am trying to do, and then maybe you could redraw to make it look good.

Randall: Okay.

Ms. S: So, see these squiggly lines between the magnet and you? That is the *magnetic force* (smiling) that pulls you into pushing other people who tease you.

Randall: Like I'm getting zapped?

Ms. S: Yep. Well, anyway, if I draw the magnet with lots of lines, you know like it is really strong and hard to resist, we could call that magnet "Boston" or "lunch line." But over here (drawing it again, down the page) we will put less lines and I'll write, "My brother is teasing me." This seemed to pull you into a "shut up" response rather than a pushing response. Now I'm wondering (drawing one more at the bottom page with a dotted line representing the "force") if we assume this is a really weak magnet, one you just ignore, what could we write to describe this situation? You know, what time did someone call you a name . . . but it was so weak . . . you just ignored it!

Randall: Oh I know. Like I was in my driveway practicing . . . and Rakita walked by and said something like, "You're no Michael Jordon" and then laughed and called me "lead butt." I just laughed and kept on shooting.

Ms. S: Outstanding. So, we'll call this one "Rakita." So, see, here there are three different situations and they seem to have different magnetic strengths. Boy, if we could help you treat them all like you did with Rakita, you would be *nonmagnetic* (laughing)!

Randall: I could do that.

Reflection "in" Practice

Randall seems to be following and is into the concept. What homework might you ask him to do?

(Continued)

(Continued)

Ms. Schulman is really impressed with Randall's engagement and wants to see if he can work on building the hierarchy.

Ms. S: Randall, you really have been a super help by remembering all these different situations when you pushed somebody in response to name-calling. I am wondering if we used this fantastic drawing (smiling) and we called this one, "Rakita" with magnet force 1 power, and this one we'll call "lunch line" with magnet force 10 power, if you could try to come up with situations that had other magnet forces between 1 to 10?

Randall: I don't know if I could find that many.

Ms. S: Oh, you don't have to find one for all ten powers. If we could remember a couple of situations when the name-calling really seemed to get you, and then a couple of situations when it started to get to you, but you didn't push the other person, and maybe a couple, like with Rakita, when it had very, very little strength, that would be great.

Randall: I could do that . . . can I redraw the pictures?

Ms. S: What, you don't like my artistic renderings (laughing)?

Randall: No, they are great. I just think it would be fun to do.

Ms. S: You're the best! See you Monday, okay?

Randall: Okay.

Reflection "on" Practice

Well, it appears that Ms. S and Randall have made quite a bit of headway. Assuming Randall is successful at finding situations when he has a variety of responses, ranging from ignoring to pushing, what might your approach for intervention be?

Ms. Schulman is very happy with the work and the working alliance she now has with Randall. She hopes he can bring a couple of examples, but even if he doesn't, she feels that she can begin to suggest a hierarchy. Her first goal will be to have Randall discuss the type of response he would like to have at the various levels. She figures a good point to start that discussion might be around the basketball example. She feels once she can identify a desirable response, then she can start the process of teaching by way of modeling, role-play, rehearsal, etc.

Third Session

(We pick up the session in the middle after Randall's illustrations have been discussed.)

Ms. S: So, we have some really good examples of different *magnet* strengths...(smiling) and by the way, I think my drawings are just as good! It seems that the strongest pull to get you to push someone is when you are in front of other students and someone is calling you a name.

Randall: Like in the bathroom or lunch line...everybody was laughing at me and I guess I just wanted to show them.

Ms. S: Okay. So up here, where the "force" is really strong, we will write the words "others looking on and calling me weak and scared." Now down here, where the magnet is really weak—like it almost doesn't even exist—I see you put Rakita, and now also another one—with Ramone? Could you tell me about that?

Randall: We were doing an experiment in science class and I knocked over the liquid. Ramone laughed and called me a weenie...

Ms. S: So he called you a name, but you have it low in force? How come?

Randall: Well, I know he was just kidding and I really did mess it up...so we were both laughing.

Ms. S: Okay, so times when you know you are messing up or when you are not really messing up, but the other people are just playing with you, those times are weak in force and you don't push them?

Randall: Yeah, it's just joking around.

Ms. S: Wow, that's great. How do you act in those situations?

Randall: Well, with Ramone, I just kind of laughed, and said yep I messed that up, so next time you can do it...and he laughed.

Ms. S: And that worked?

Randall: Worked?

Ms. S: I mean, what happened after you said that?

Randall: Well, he laughed and we got back to work.

Ms. S: So, it worked. You had fun and didn't get sent to Dr. Kim, or get in any trouble, and you went back to work. Did the same thing happen when Rakita said you were no Michael Jordon and that you were...I think you said...(smiling) a "lead butt"?

(Continued)

(Continued)

Randall: Yeah, I guess. I just laughed and told her that I would play her any time. She just laughed and said something, but I don't remember what it was.

Ms. S: So, you really have the ability to just play with the comment and not take it seriously, and just get back to doing what you were doing, like the science project and the basketball? Super. Now, how about here (pointing to the middle magnet)? You have your brother calling you "shrimp" while you were playing b'ball. How did you handle that?

Randall: I called him a bad name . . . but then just kept playing.

Ms. S: So, he got you a little mad but you didn't push him, great. Is that what happened here with Alfred?

Randall: I guess. We were in English class and I was giving a book report, and my voice cracked, and when I was walking back Alfred said I sounded like a girl . . . I just looked at him and said something like "I'll show you who's a girl" . . . and went to my seat.

Ms. S: Okay, so how do you explain that these magnets are a little stronger, but not as strong as the ones at the top?

Randall: I don't know . . . except only nobody else was around . . . I mean even with Alfred, he said it softly so only I heard it.

Ms. S: Okay. So, when you know you messed up and you know the other person is just playing around, you are cool . . . and if someone is trying to get you upset but only you hear it, you seem to be able to respond without pushing. Good. You just say something and move on. Good for you!

Randall: Yeah, I guess so. But this stuff up here is hard to just play with (pointing higher on the list, with examples of Boston in the lunch line and the bathroom incident).

Ms. S: Yeah, I bet they are. These are situations where it seems someone is trying to push your button and they are doing it in front of other students. But how do you feel if you could just react like you did with Alfred, or better yet, just laugh and keep on doing your thing like you did with Ramone?

Randall: I wouldn't get in trouble as much, but I don't know if I could do that.

Ms. S: Maybe not right now. But with practice, I bet you could. Just think about your basketball. I bet when you first saw some of the older kids playing b'ball, you couldn't do some of things they did . . . but I bet you can now.

Randall:	Yeah, I got some of the little guys at the center trying to be like me!
Ms. S:	I'm impressed! But how did you go from not being able to do it, (smiling) to now being a "star"?
Randall:	I practiced a lot. I'm always in the driveway or in the center practicing.
Ms. S:	Same thing here. I bet if we practice, you could get really good at ignoring these comments and reducing the power of the magnet (smiling).
Randall:	How?
Ms. S:	Well, how about we get together tomorrow and I'll explain what we can do, and if you are up to it, then we'll do it. Okay?
Randall:	At lunchtime?
Ms. S:	If that's okay with you?
Randall:	See you tomorrow.

Reflection "on" Practice

As you think about the upcoming session, what would your intervention plan involve? Would you use the situations presented and have Randall model your response? Would you employ some form of mental image to help him? Or covert that he could use to guide his reactions? How about reinforcement for employing this new behavior?

Ms. Schulman appreciates the enthusiasm and real sense of ownership that Randall has displayed. She plans to use role-play and rehearsal as ways to develop alternative response patterns to varying situations. The elements she is targeting are:

1. Situations where he accepts he is doing okay, or has messed up and assumes the other person is just playing (low strength).

2. Situations in which he feels the person may be trying to push his button, but it's just the two of them with no audience (peers) (medium strength).

3. Situations in which he has an audience of peers and feels the other is trying to make him look silly or put him down in some fashion (high strength).

She thinks she will practice with the medium strength and attempt to identify ways of responding that will allow Randall to feel okay at the moment and continue doing what it is he was doing or about to do.

(Continued)

(Continued)

Fourth Session

(This session picks up after initial "social" exchanges.)

Ms. S: Okay. Did you think about some of the things we talked about? You know, ignoring comments and reducing the strength of those magnets (smiling)?

Randall: Yeah, I know those things are dumb. But I just flip out sometimes. It's like I can't help myself.

Ms. S: Maybe that's because you need a little practice . . . on handling these situations. And, I bet if we practiced with these types of things you may even begin to use the same approach when Boston and those guys try to get into it with you?

Randall: I don't know.

Ms. S: Well, we'll worry about that later. But for now, maybe you could explain something to me. When you play basketball and it's a really close game, and you get fouled, do you do anything to calm yourself down and focus before you shoot the winning foul shot?

Randall: Yeah, usually I take a deep breath and tell myself to slow down and relax. Then, I dribble three times at the line and shoot. My brother told me about the breathing thing.

Reflection "in" Practice

It appears that Randall has a set of behaviors in his repertoire that could be used to reduce his level of anger when others attempt to push his button. How would you begin to expand on this coping skill?

Ms Schulman recognizes that this calming response could be useful when Randall has these encounters that have, to date, aroused anger and then resulted in the pushing behavior. She wants to see if Randall will embrace the value of the strategy.

Ms. S: That's a super strategy. I wonder if it would work in situations where people are trying to push your button. You know, like if Alfred is saying something about your voice cracking. I wonder what would happen if you took a deep breath and told yourself to slow down, relax.

Randall: I don't know.

Ms. S: Well, let's try something. I'll be Alfred and you can close your eyes and try to imagine being back in class and just finishing your presentation. Now, when you see yourself walking down the aisle to your seat, I will make a comment, but this time I want you to stop and simply take a breath when you hear my comment, and then say to yourself, "slow down, relax." Could you try that?

Randall: I guess.

Ms. S: Okay, so . . . maybe you could close your eyes so you could really see the classroom. Okay, so you just finished and the teacher said, "Well done." Now you are walking back to your seat and you see some of the other kids in your class . . . like there's Boston, and Lilly and Thomas, and now you are passing Alfred and you go to your seat. As you pass him, he says, "Hey loser . . . nice voice . . . really girly like." Now stop . . . take a breath, remind yourself to slow down . . . relax . . . good. Good, keep it up. Now see yourself moving past him and to your seat. Okay, open your eyes.

Well? What happened? How do you feel?

Randall: You really sounded like Alfred . . . (smiling) calling me a loser.

Ms. S: But, did you notice anything when I said that?

Randall: Yeah, I started to get pumped up.

Ms. S: Okay. But when I reminded you to take a breath and say to yourself slow down . . . what happened?

Randall: For some reason I thought about basketball . . . and I guess I slowed down, but I wasn't thinking about Alfred, I mean you, cuttin' me up. I guess I calmed down.

Ms. S: Neat. Let's try it again, but this time, as we do it, I will tell you to pay attention to a couple of things. Okay?

Randall: Sure.

Ms. S: Okay. Close your eyes and take a minute to try to see the room. Now, you just finished and the teacher said, "Good job." As you start to walk back you see Lilly, she's right in front . . . then you see Alfred. Now stop. Don't open your eyes, but do you feel yourself getting a little tense?

Randall: (Nods yes.)

(Continued)

(Continued)

Ms. S: Okay. And now as you pass, he whispers "Loser . . . nice voice . . . really girly." Okay . . . now focus on your instruction . . . say to yourself, "take a breath . . . slow down . . . move on."

(Waits.)

Open your eyes . . . how did you do?

Randall: Well, it's funny. When you stopped me and asked if I was getting tense, I was, and I was thinking about what you were going to say . . . but it's weird . . . my brain said relax, take a breath, chill even before you said it! So, I really wasn't paying attention to you when you called me a loser.

Ms. S: You are spectacular! See, just a couple of practices and you are already starting to get into the process. In fact, I like what you did when you said, "relax . . . breathe . . . chill."

Randall: Yeah, it just kind of went off in my head.

Ms. S: Kind of like a button was pushed, but rather than the "push the other guy button" it was the "relax, breathe, chill" button?

Randall: Yeah.

Ms. S: Fantastic.

Reflection "in" Practice

As we come to the end of this session, what "homework" assignment might you suggest?

Ms. Schulman feels Randall has embraced the concept and sees the value of calming, at least in basketball, so she is going to get him to practice the behavior at basketball, and then perhaps at a medium level trigger-type event.

Ms. S: Would you try practicing that phrase—you know, "relax, breathe, chill"—for the next couple of days?

Randall: Practice . . . where?

Ms. S: Well, it may be good to use at the foul line when you are playing b'ball.

Randall: Yeah, I could that. We have games this weekend.

Ms. S: But I'm wondering if there are situations that may come up over the weekend where somebody may try to tease you or push your button and you could use it then?

Randall: Well, I know my brother and his friends will be over and they usually try to get me pumped by calling me "shrimp," or "stick legs" or . . . and this usually gets me angry "MWB."

Ms. S: MWB?

Randall: Michael-wanna-be! They think I'm trying to act like Michael Jordon.

Ms. S: Oh, and that pushes your button?

Randall: Sometimes.

Ms. S: Okay. For homework, how about over the weekend, anytime you are at the foul line, you will say to yourself, "relax, breathe, and chill"! And maybe, even when your brother's friends try to tease you, maybe even then you could try using your new button, the "relax, breathe, chill" button?

Randall: I'll try!

Reflection "on" Practice

If you envisioned two more formal sessions with Randall, what would be your specific objectives for each session, and what strategies would you employ?

As Ms. Schulman reflects on her work with Randall, she begins laying out a tentative plan that includes:

1. Ask Randall to review homework and, if successful, practice with a trigger higher on the hierarchy. If not successful, use the specific scenario experienced over the weekend to practice in session.

2. If progress is evident, suggest that Randall take a week or two and try employing his new button response at games, at home, and here at school. Ask him to journal about the results.

3. If little progress is made, meet in three days with Randall to practice either the simulated cases he provided or review his lived experience and use those for further training in session.

Fifth Session

We pick up the fifth session near the end of the session. Randall has provided four different situations, two during basketball games and two with his brother

(Continued)

(Continued)

and friends, where he was able to use the new strategy. In reviewing the impact, it became clear that not only was Randall able to stay calm and not overreact, but he also has a wealth of funny and socially appropriate comebacks in these situations. It appears that, in the past, he was unable to use these social skills because his anger interfered with their retrieval.

Ms. S: So, what do you think? Pretty amazing, huh? Not only did you stay calm, but also you were able to have some fun with the older guys—cutting up!

Randall: Yeah, that was cool . . . but the best was when Charles was trying to get me all angry during the game. At one point, I was dribbling and he was behind me mouthing off and I kept saying "chill, relax," and I faked him out of his shorts. Everybody went nuts!

Ms. S: So, chilling . . . staying relaxed, really does work!

Randall: Yeah, it was so cool.

Ms. S: Well, you really have done a super job. I would like to try something. I would like to have you practice using your new button of relax, breathe, and chill for maybe a week . . . you know, at your games and at home with your brother and here at school. And then we can check with each other to see how's it going? What do you think? Maybe you could even keep some of these in your journal and bring that with you?

Randall: Yeah, okay. But could I stop in—if something happens?

Ms. S: Absolutely. I'm here. And you can stop in even if something doesn't happen (smiling), but for now, let's get you back to English class!

Reflection "on" Practice

Randall has certainly grabbed on to the concept of using his deep breathing and private reminder to relax and chill. As you reflect on your work with Randall, what is your plan for your next meeting? What specific goals might you have for the next session and what would your approach be?

Ms. Schulman really believes that Randall is invested in practicing his new response pattern, but she has a concern whether he will be able to engage this alternative response if he encounters another public confrontation like he had in the bathroom or at lunch. As she thinks about seeing him in a week or so, she decides it may be worthwhile to "wander down" to lunch in a couple of days just to do a check-in and reinforce his good work. As for the next meeting, she's planning on one of two strategies:

1. If Randall shows that he is doing well and has examples of where he used the strategy under more intense situations, then she would plan on moving toward termination of this contract. She is aware that Randall enjoys working with her so she wants to find that balance between being available and supportive while discouraging his desire to simply "hang out." She thinks maybe a couple of "informal" contacts at lunch where she could engage Randall and his friends might be a way to shift the focus from Randall, to the small group.

2. If Randall shares that he had some difficulty with employing the strategy, then she will create full descriptions of the situations that were problematic and practice with him using these images. She may also check to see if maybe some stickers, maybe little basketball stickers, could be used as visual reminders for him to practice. She could have him put a couple on his binder or bag and hopefully he could see these when he is at lunch; these would provide the cue that he may need to keep chilled if something comes up.

Epilogue

A Beginning . . . Not an End

While we have come to the end of this book, it is hopefully only the beginning of your own ongoing development as a reflective school counselor. The material presented in this book has provided you with an introduction to the world of a behavioral school counselor, and the procedural thinking that guides his or her practice. However, it is truly just the beginning.

As school counselors, we know the value of maintaining competence in the skills we use and we know the ethical mandate to continue to develop those skills (see Resource, Standard E.1.c). While being open to new procedures demonstrated to be effective for the diverse population with whom we work, we must also recognize the limitations of our professional competence to use these procedures (see Resource, Standard E.1.a). The material provided in this book is but a first step to developing that competency.

Becoming an expert in counseling, as is true of any profession, requires continued training, personal reflection, and supervision. It is hoped that with this introduction to the theory and practice of a behavioral counselor, you will be stimulated to continue in that training, personal reflection, and supervision and as a result grow in thinking and acting like an expert.

Resource

*Ethical Standards
for School Counselors*

The American School Counselor Association's (ASCA) Ethical Standards for School Counselors were adopted by the ASCA Delegate Assembly, March 19,1984, revised March 27, 1992, June 25, 1998 and June 26, 2004. For a PDF version of the Ethical Standards visit www.schoolcounselor.org/content.asp?contentid=173.

PREAMBLE

The American School Counselor Association (ASCA) is a professional organization whose members are certified/licensed in school counseling with unique qualifications and skills to address the academic, personal/social, and career development needs of all students. Professional school counselors are advocates, leaders, collaborators, and consultants who create opportunities for equity in access and success in educational opportunities by connecting their programs to the mission of schools and subscribing to the following tenets of professional responsibility:

- Each person has the right to be respected, be treated with dignity, and have access to a comprehensive school counseling program that advocates for and affirms all students from diverse populations regardless of ethnic/racial status, age, economic status, special needs, English as a second language or other language group, immigration status, sexual orientation, gender, gender identity/expression, family type, religious/spiritual identity, and appearance.
- Each person has the right to receive the information and support needed to move toward self-direction and self-development and affirmation within one's group identities, with special care being

given to students who have historically not received adequate educational services: students of color, low socioeconomic students, students with disabilities and students with nondominant language backgrounds.

- Each person has the right to understand the full magnitude and meaning of his or her educational choices and how those choices will affect future opportunities.

- Each person has the right to privacy and thereby the right to expect the counselor-student relationship to comply with all laws, policies, and ethical standards pertaining to confidentiality in the school setting.

In this document, ASCA specifies the principles of ethical behavior necessary to maintain the high standards of integrity, leadership, and professionalism among its members. The Ethical Standards for School Counselors were developed to clarify the nature of ethical responsibilities held in common by school counseling professionals. The purposes of this document are to:

- Serve as a guide for the ethical practices of all professional school counselors regardless of level, area, population served or membership in this professional association.

- Provide self-appraisal and peer evaluations regarding counselor responsibilities to students, parents/guardians, colleagues, and professional associates, schools, communities, and the counseling profession.

- Inform those served by the school counselor of acceptable counselor practices and expected professional behavior.

A.1. Responsibilities to Students

The professional school counselor:

a. Has a primary obligation to the student, who is to be treated with respect as a unique individual.

b. Is concerned with the educational, academic, career, personal, and social needs and encourages the maximum development of every student.

c. Respects the student's values and beliefs and does not impose the counselor's personal values.

d. Is knowledgeable of laws, regulations, and policies relating to students and strives to protect and inform students regarding their rights.

A.2. Confidentiality

The professional school counselor:

a. Informs students of the purposes, goals, techniques, and rules of procedure under which they may receive counseling at or before the time when the counseling relationship is entered. Disclosure notice includes the limits of confidentiality such as the possible necessity for consulting with other professionals, privileged communication, and legal or authoritative restraints. The meaning and limits of confidentiality are defined in developmentally appropriate terms to students.

b. Keeps information confidential unless disclosure is required to prevent clear and imminent danger to the student or others or when legal requirements demand that confidential information be revealed. Counselors will consult with appropriate professionals when in doubt as to the validity of an exception.

c. In absence of state legislation expressly forbidding disclosure, considers the ethical responsibility to provide information to an identified third party who, by his or her relationship with the student, is at a high risk of contracting a disease that is commonly known to be communicable and fatal. Disclosure requires satisfaction of all of the following conditions:
   - Student identifies partner or the partner is highly identifiable.
   - Counselor recommends the student notify partner and refrain from further high-risk behavior.
   - Student refuses.
   - Counselor informs the student of the intent to notify the partner.
   - Counselor seeks legal consultation as to the legalities of informing the partner.

d. Requests of the court that disclosure not be required when the release of confidential information may potentially harm a student or the counseling relationship.

e. Protects the confidentiality of students' records and releases personal data in accordance with prescribed laws and school policies. Student information stored and transmitted electronically is treated with the same care as traditional student records.

f. Protects the confidentiality of information received in the counseling relationship as specified by federal and state laws, written policies, and applicable ethical standards. Such information is only to be revealed to others with the informed consent of the student, consistent with the counselor's ethical obligation.

g. Recognizes his or her primary obligation for confidentiality is to the student but balances that obligation with an understanding of the legal and inherent rights of parents/guardians to be the guiding voice in their children's lives.

A.3. Counseling Plans

The professional school counselor:

a. Provides students with a comprehensive school counseling program that includes a strong emphasis on working jointly with all students to develop academic and career goals.

b. Advocates for counseling plans supporting students right to choose from the wide array of options when they leave secondary education. Such plans will be regularly reviewed to update students regarding critical information they need to make informed decisions.

A.4. Dual Relationships

The professional school counselor:

a. Avoids dual relationships that might impair his or her objectivity and increase the risk of harm to the student (e.g., counseling one's family members, close friends, or associates). If a dual relationship is unavoidable, the counselor is responsible for taking action to eliminate or reduce the potential for harm. Such safeguards might include informed consent, consultation, supervision, and documentation.

b. Avoids dual relationships with school personnel that might infringe on the integrity of the counselor/student relationship.

A.5. Appropriate Referrals

The professional school counselor:

a. Makes referrals when necessary or appropriate to outside resources. Appropriate referrals may necessitate informing both parents/guardians and students of applicable resources and making proper plans for transitions with minimal interruption of services. Students retain the right to discontinue the counseling relationship at any time.

A.6. Group Work

The professional school counselor:

a. Screens prospective group members and maintains an awareness of participants' needs and goals in relation to the goals of the group. The counselor takes reasonable precautions to protect members from physical and psychological harm resulting from interaction within the group.

b. Notifies parents/guardians and staff of group participation if the counselor deems it appropriate and if consistent with school board policy or practice.

c. Establishes clear expectations in the group setting and clearly states that confidentiality in group counseling cannot be guaranteed. Given the developmental and chronological ages of minors in schools, the counselor recognizes the tenuous nature of confidentiality for minors renders some topics inappropriate for group work in a school setting.

d. Follows up with group members and documents proceedings as appropriate.

A.7. Danger to Self or Others

The professional school counselor:

a. Informs parents/guardians or appropriate authorities when the student's condition indicates a clear and imminent danger to the student or others. This is to be done after careful deliberation and, where possible, after consultation with other counseling professionals.

b. Will attempt to minimize threat to a student and may choose to (1) inform the student of actions to be taken, (2) involve the student in a three-way communication with parents/guardians when breaching confidentiality, or (3) allow the student to have input as to how and to whom the breach will be made.

A.8. Student Records

The professional school counselor:

a. Maintains and secures records necessary for rendering professional services to the student as required by laws, regulations, institutional procedures, and confidentiality guidelines.

b. Keeps sole-possession records separate from students' educational records in keeping with state laws.

c. Recognizes the limits of sole-possession records and understands these records are a memory aid for the creator and in absence of privilege communication may be subpoenaed and may become educational records when they (1) are shared with others in verbal or written form, (2) include information other than professional opinion or personal observations, and/or (3) are made accessible to others.

d. Establishes a reasonable timeline for purging sole-possession records or case notes. Suggested guidelines include shredding sole-possession records when the student transitions to the next level, transfers to another school, or graduates. Careful discretion and deliberation should be applied before destroying sole-possession records that may be needed by a court of law such as notes on child abuse, suicide, sexual harassment, or violence.

A.9. Evaluation, Assessment, and Interpretation

The professional school counselor:

a. Adheres to all professional standards regarding selecting, administering, and interpreting assessment measures and only utilizes assessment measures that are within the scope of practice for school counselors.

b. Seeks specialized training regarding the use of electronically-based testing programs in administering, scoring, and interpreting that may differ from that required in more traditional assessments.

c. Considers confidentiality issues when utilizing evaluative or assessment instruments and electronically-based programs.

d. Provides interpretation of the nature, purposes, results, and potential impact of assessment/evaluation measures in language the student(s) can understand.

e. Monitors the use of assessment results and interpretations, and takes reasonable steps to prevent others from misusing the information.

f. Uses caution when utilizing assessment techniques, making evaluations, and interpreting the performance of populations not represented in the norm group on which an instrument is standardized.

g. Assesses the effectiveness of his or her program in having an impact on students' academic, career, and personal/social development through accountability measures especially examining efforts to close achievement, opportunity, and attainment gaps.

A.10. Technology

The professional school counselor:

a. Promotes the benefits of and clarifies the limitations of various appropriate technological applications. The counselor promotes technological applications (1) that are appropriate for the student's individual needs, (2) that the student understands how to use and (3) for which follow-up counseling assistance is provided.

b. Advocates for equal access to technology for all students, especially those historically underserved.

c. Takes appropriate and reasonable measures for maintaining confidentiality of student information and educational records stored or transmitted over electronic media including although not limited to fax, electronic mail, and instant messaging.

d. While working with students on a computer or similar technology, takes reasonable and appropriate measures to protect students from objectionable and/or harmful online material.

e. Who is engaged in the delivery of services involving technologies such as the telephone, videoconferencing, and the Internet takes responsible steps to protect students and others from harm.

A.11. Student Peer Support Program

The professional school counselor:

Has unique responsibilities when working with student-assistance programs. The school counselor is responsible for the welfare of students participating in peer-to-peer programs under his or her direction.

B. RESPONSIBILITIES TO PARENTS/GUARDIANS

B.1. Parent Rights and Responsibilities

The professional school counselor:

a. Respects the rights and responsibilities of parents/guardians for their children and endeavors to establish, as appropriate, a collaborative relationship with parents/guardians to facilitate the student's maximum development.

b. Adheres to laws, local guidelines, and ethical standards of practice when assisting parents/guardians experiencing family difficulties that interfere with the student's effectiveness and welfare.

c. Respects the confidentiality of parents/guardians.

d. Is sensitive to diversity among families and recognizes that all parents/guardians, custodial and noncustodial, are vested with certain rights and responsibilities for the welfare of their children by virtue of their role and according to law.

B.2. Parents/Guardians and Confidentiality

The professional school counselor:

a. Informs parents/guardians of the counselor's role with emphasis on the confidential nature of the counseling relationship between the counselor and student.

b. Recognizes that working with minors in a school setting may require counselors to collaborate with students' parents/guardians.

c. Provides parents/guardians with accurate, comprehensive, and relevant information in an objective and caring manner, as is appropriate and consistent with ethical responsibilities to the student.

d. Makes reasonable efforts to honor the wishes of parents/guardians concerning information regarding the student, and in cases of divorce or separation exercises a good-faith effort to keep both parents informed with regard to critical information with the exception of a court order.

C. RESPONSIBILITIES TO COLLEAGUES AND PROFESSIONAL ASSOCIATES

C.1. Professional Relationships

The professional school counselor:

a. Establishes and maintains professional relationships with faculty, staff, and administration to facilitate an optimum counseling program.

b. Treats colleagues with professional respect, courtesy, and fairness. The qualifications, views, and findings of colleagues are represented to accurately reflect the image of competent professionals.

c. Is aware of and utilizes related professionals, organizations, and other resources to whom the student may be referred.

C.2. Sharing Information With Other Professionals

The professional school counselor:

a. Promotes awareness and adherence to appropriate guidelines regarding confidentiality, the distinction between public and private information and staff consultation.

b. Provides professional personnel with accurate, objective, concise, and meaningful data necessary to adequately evaluate, counsel, and assist the student.

c. If a student is receiving services from another counselor or other mental health professional, the counselor, with student and/or parent/ guardian consent, will inform the other professional and develop clear agreements to avoid confusion and conflict for the student.

d. Is knowledgeable about release of information and parental rights in sharing information.

D. RESPONSIBILITIES TO THE SCHOOL AND COMMUNITY

D.1. Responsibilities to the School

The professional school counselor:

a. Supports and protects the educational program against any infringement not in students' best interest.

b. Informs appropriate officials in accordance with school policy of conditions that may be potentially disruptive or damaging to the school's mission, personnel, and property while honoring the confidentiality between the student and counselor.

c. Is knowledgeable and supportive of the school's mission and connects his or her program to the school's mission.

d. Delineates and promotes the counselor's role and function in meeting the needs of those served. Counselors will notify appropriate officials of conditions that may limit or curtail their effectiveness in providing programs and services.

e. Accepts employment only for positions for which he or she is qualified by education, training, supervised experience, state and national professional credentials, and appropriate professional experience.

f. Advocates that administrators hire only qualified and competent individuals for professional counseling positions.

g. Assists in developing: (1) curricular and environmental conditions appropriate for the school and community, (2) educational procedures and programs to meet students' developmental needs and (3) a systematic evaluation process for comprehensive, developmental, standards-based school counseling programs, services, and personnel. The counselor is guided by the findings of the evaluation data in planning programs and services.

D.2. Responsibility to the Community

The professional school counselor:

a. Collaborates with agencies, organizations and individuals in the community in the best interest of students and without regard to personal reward or remuneration.

b. Extends his or her influence and opportunity to deliver a comprehensive school counseling program to all students by collaborating with community resources for student success.

E. RESPONSIBILITIES TO SELF

E.1. Professional Competence

The professional school counselor:

a. Functions within the boundaries of individual professional competence and accepts responsibility for the consequences of his or her actions.

b. Monitors personal well-being and effectiveness and does not participate in any activity that may lead to inadequate professional services or harm to a student.

c. Strives through personal initiative to maintain professional competence including technological literacy and to keep abreast of professional information. Professional and personal growth are ongoing throughout the counselor's career.

E.2. Diversity

The professional school counselor:

a. Affirms the diversity of students, staff, and families.

b. Expands and develops awareness of his or her own attitudes and beliefs affecting cultural values and biases and strives to attain cultural competence.

c. Possesses knowledge and understanding about how oppression, racism, discrimination, and stereotyping affects her or him personally and professionally.

d. Acquires educational, consultation, and training experiences to improve awareness, knowledge, skills, and effectiveness in working with diverse populations: ethnic/racial status, age, economic status, special needs, ESL or ELL, immigration status, sexual orientation, gender, gender identity/expression, family type, religious/spiritual identity, and appearance.

F. RESPONSIBILITIES TO THE PROFESSION

F.1. Professionalism

The professional school counselor:

a. Accepts the policies and procedures for handling ethical violations as a result of maintaining membership in the American School Counselor Association.

b. Conducts herself or himself in such a manner as to advance individual ethical practice and the profession.

c. Conducts appropriate research and report findings in a manner consistent with acceptable educational and psychological research practices. The counselor advocates for the protection of the individual student's identity when using data for research or program planning.

d. Adheres to ethical standards of the profession, other official policy statements, such as ASCA's position statements, role statement, and the ASCA National Model, and relevant statutes established by federal, state and local governments, and when these are in conflict works responsibly for change.

e. Clearly distinguishes between statements and actions made as a private individual and those made as a representative of the school counseling profession.

f. Does not use his or her professional position to recruit or gain clients, consultees for his or her private practice or to seek and receive unjustified personal gains, unfair advantage, inappropriate relationships, or unearned goods or services.

F.2. Contribution to the Profession

The professional school counselor:

a. Actively participates in local, state, and national associations fostering the development and improvement of school counseling.

b. Contributes to the development of the profession through the sharing of skills, ideas, and expertise with colleagues.

c. Provides support and mentoring to novice professionals.

G. Maintenance of Standards

Ethical behavior among professional school counselors, association members and nonmembers, is expected at all times. When there exists serious doubt as to the ethical behavior of colleagues or if counselors are forced to work in situations or abide by policies that do not reflect the standards as outlined in these Ethical Standards for School Counselors, the counselor is obligated to take appropriate action to rectify the condition. The following procedure may serve as a guide:

1. The counselor should consult confidentially with a professional colleague to discuss the nature of a complaint to see if the professional colleague views the situation as an ethical violation.

2. When feasible, the counselor should directly approach the colleague whose behavior is in question to discuss the complaint and seek resolution.

3. If resolution is not forthcoming at the personal level, the counselor shall utilize the channels established within the school, school district, the state school counseling association, and ASCA's Ethics Committee.

4. If the matter still remains unresolved, referral for review and appropriate action should be made to the Ethics Committees in the following sequence:

   - state school counselor association
   - American School Counselor Association

5. The ASCA Ethics Committee is responsible for:

   - educating and consulting with the membership regarding ethical standards.
   - periodically reviewing and recommending changes in code
   - receiving and processing questions to clarify the application of such standards; questions must be submitted in writing to the ASCA Ethics chair.
   - handling complaints of alleged violations of the ethical standards. At the national level, complaints should be submitted in writing to the ASCA Ethics Committee, c/o the Executive Director.

SOURCE: American School Counselor Association. Used with permission.

References

Barrios, B. A., & O'Dell, S. L. (1998). Fears and anxieties. In E. J. Mash and R. A. Barkley (Eds.), *Treatment of childhood disorders* (2nd ed.) (pp. 249–337). New York: Guildford Press.

Bryan, T., & Sullivan-Burstein, K. (1998). Teacher-selected strategies for improving homework completion. *Remedial & Special Education, 19* (5), 263–276.

Carlson, C. L., Mann, M., & Alexander, D. K. (2000). Effects of rewards and response cost on the performance and motivation of children with ADHD. *Cognitive Therapy and Research, 24,* 87–98.

Carter, S. (1994). Organizing systems to support competent social behavior in children and youth. *Interventions.* ERIC Document Services NO: ED380971.

Chi, M. T. H., Feltovich, P. J., & Glaser, R. (1981). Categorization and representation of physics problems by experts and novices. *Cognitive Science, 5,* 121–152.

Duhon, G. J., Noell, G. H., Witt, J. C., Freeland, J. T., Dufrene, B. A., Gilbertson, D. N. (2004). Identifying academic skill and performance deficits: The experimental analysis of brief assessments of academic skills. *School Psychology Review, 33* (3), 429–443.

Evans, S. W., Axelrod, J., & Langberg, J. M. (2004). Efficacy of a school-based treatment program for middle school youth with ADHD. *Behavior Modification, 28,* 528–547.

Everett, G. E., Olmi, D. J., Edwards, R. P., Tingstrom, D. H., Sterling-Turner, H. E., & Christ, T. J. (2007). An empirical investigation of time-out with and without escape extinction to treat escape-maintained noncompliance. *Behavior Modification, 31* (4), 412–434.

Fiore, T. A., Becker, E. A., Nero, R. C. (1993). Educational interventions for students with attention deficit disorder. *Exceptional Children, 60* (2), 163–173.

Franklin, M. E., Tolin, D. F., March, J. S., & Foa, E. B. (2001). Treatment of pediatric obsessive-compulsive disorder: A case example of intensive cognitive-behavioral therapy involving exposure and ritual prevention. *Cognitive and Behavioral Practice, 8,* 297–304.

Hoshmand, L. T. (1994). Supervision of predoctoral graduate research: A practice-oriented approach. *Counseling Psychologist, 22* (1), 147–162.

Irving, J. A., & Williamson, D. I. (1995). Critical thinking and reflective practice in counseling. *British Journal of Guidance and Counseling, 23* (1), 107–116.

Jacobson, E. (1938). *Progressive relaxation.* Chicago: University of Chicago Press.

Jenson, W. R., Sloane, H., & Young, R. (1988). *Token economies. Applied behavior analysis in education: A structured teaching approach.* New York: Prentice Hall.

Jones, R. N., & Downing, R. H. (1991). Assessment of the use of time-out in an inpatient child psychiatry treatment unit. *Behavioral Residential Treatment, 6,* 219–230.

Kazdin, A. E. (2001). *Behavior modification in applied settings* (6th ed.). Pacific Grove, CA: Brooks-Cole.

Kelly, M. L., & Stokes, T. F. (1984). Student-teacher contracting with goal setting for maintenance. *Behavior Modification, 8,* 223–244.

King, N. J., & Ollendick, T. H. (1998). Empirically validated treatments in clinical psychology. *Australian Psychologist, 33* (2), 89–95.

King, N. J., Heyne, D., Tonge, B., Gullone, E., & Ollendick, T. H. (2001). School refusal: categorical diagnoses, functional analysis and treatment planning. *Clinical Psychology & Psychotherapy, 8* (5), 352–360.

Lane, K. L., Umbreit, J., & Beebe-Frankenberger, M. E. (1999). Functional assessment research on students with or at risk for EBD: 1990 to the present. *Journal of Positive Behavior Interventions,* Spr., 101–111.

Linscheid, T. R., Pejeau, C., Cohen, S., & Footo-Lenz, M. (1994). Positive side-effects in the treatment of SIB using the Self-Injurious Behavior Inhibiting System (SIBIS): Implications for operant and biochemical explanations of SIB. *Research in Developmental Disabilities, 15,* 81–90.

MacPhee, A. R., & Andrews, J. J. W. (2003). Twelve year review of in vivo exposure: Treating specific phobias in children. *Canadian Journal of School Psychology, 18* (1–2), 183–2001.

Martell, C. R., Addis, M. E., & Jacobson, N. S. (2001). *Depression in context: Strategies for guided action.* New York: W. W. Norton & Co.

Martin, G., & Pear, J. (2003). *Behavior modification: What it is and how to do it* (7th ed.). Upper Saddle River, NJ: Prentice-Hall.

Miltenberger, R. G. (1997). *Behavior modification: Principles and procedures.* Pacific Grove, CA: Brooks-Cole.

Miltenberger, R. G. (2004). *Behavior modification: Principles and procedures* (3rd ed.). Pacific Grove, CA: Brooks-Cole.

Nelson, M. L., & Neufeldt, S. A. (1998). The pedagogy of counseling: A critical examination. *Counselor Education and Supervision, 38,* 70–88.

Olmi, D. J., Sevier, R. C., & Nastasi, D. F. (1997). Time-in/time-out as a response to noncompliance and inappropriate behavior with students with developmental disabilities: Two case studies. *Psychology in the Schools, 34* (1), 31–39.

O'Reilly, M., Lancioni, G., & Taylor, I. (1999). An empirical analysis of two forms of extinction to treat aggression. *Research in Developmental Disabilities, 20* (5), 315–325.

Parsons, R. D. (2007). *Counseling strategies that work.* Boston: Allyn & Bacon.

Pfiffner, L. J., & O'Leary, S. G. (1987). The efficacy of all-positive management as a function of the prior use of negative consequences. *Journal of Applied Behavior Analysis, 20,* 265–271.

Prochaska, J. O. & Norcross, J. C. (1994). *Systems of Psychotherapy: A Trans-theoretical Approach*. Pacific Grove, CA: Brooks-Cole.

Purdie, N., Hattie, J., & Carroll, A. (2002). A Review of the research on interventions for attention deficit hyperactivity disorder: What works best? *Review of Educational Research, 72* (1), 61–100.

Reavis, H. K., Sweeten, M. T., Jenson, W. R., Morgan, D. P., Andrews, D. J., & Fister, S. L. (1996). *BEST practices: Behavioral and educational strategies for teachers*. Longmont, CO: Sopris West.

Shukla-Mehta, S., & Albin, R. W. (2003). Twelve practical strategies to prevent behavioral escalation in classroom settings. *Clearing House, 77* (2), 50–56.

Skinner, B. F. (1971). *Beyond freedom and dignity*. New York: Knopf.

Spiegler, M. D., & Guevremont, D. C. (1998). *Contemporary behavior therapy* (3rd ed.). Belmont, CA: Brooks-Cole.

Sulzer-Azaroff, B., & Mayer, G. R. (1996). *Applying behavior-analysis procedures with children and youth*. New York: Holt, Rinehart, and Winston.

Tremmel, R. (1993). Zen and the art of reflective practice in teacher education. *Harvard Educational Review, 63* (4), 434–460.

Umbreit, J., Lane, K. L., & Dejud, C. (2004). Improving classroom behavior by modifying task difficulty: The effects of increasing the difficulty of too easy tasks. *Journal of Positive Behavior Interventions, 6,* 13–20.

Vollmer, T. R., Iwata, B. A., Zarcone, J. R., Smith, R. G., & Mazaleski, J. L. (1993). The role of attention in the treatment of attention-maintained self-injurious behavior: Noncontingent reinforcement and differential reinforcement of other behavior. *Journal of Applied Behavior Analysis, 26* (1), 9–21.

Walker, H. M. (1995). *The acting-out child: Coping with classroom disruption* (2nd ed.). Longmont, CO: Sopris West.

Whitlock, E. P., Orleans, C. T., Pender, N. & Allan, J. (2002). Evaluating primary care behavioral counseling interventions: An evidence-based approach. *American Journal of Preventive Medicine, 22* (4), 267–284.

Wierzbicki, M. (1999). *Introduction to clinical psychology: Scientific foundation to clinical practice*. Needham Heights, MA: Allyn & Bacon.

Wilkinson, L. A. (2003). Using behavioral consultation to reduce challenging behavior in the classroom. *Preventing School Failure, 47* (3), 100–105.

Wolpe, J. (1958). *Psychotherapy by reciprocal inhibition*. Stanford, CA: Stanford University Press.

Index

CORWIN

A SAGE Company

The Corwin logo—a raven striding across an open book—represents the union of courage and learning. Corwin is committed to improving education for all learners by publishing books and other professional development resources for those serving the field of PreK–12 education. By providing practical, hands-on materials, Corwin continues to carry out the promise of its motto: **"Helping Educators Do Their Work Better."**